# 12
# TINY
# THINGS

# 12
# TINY
# THINGS

## Simple Ways to Live
## a More Intentional Life

Heidi Barr and Ellie Roscher

 Broadleaf Books

Minneapolis

12 TINY THINGS
Simple Ways to Live a More Intentional Life

Some names of people have been changed to protect privacy.

Cover design: Lindsey Owens
Heidi Barr author photo © Brian Bradley
Ellie Roscher author photo © Juliet Farmer

Print ISBN: 978-1-5064-6504-3
eBook ISBN: 978-1-5064-6505-0

*For the powerful female healers in my life: Tina Green, Michele Rae, Susan Vaughn-Fier, and Tricia Spitzmueller—who have accompanied me toward wholeness one tiny step at a time. —ER*

*For my brothers: Jacob, Andrew, and Alexander Helling. —HB*

Maybe you are searching in the branches for what only exists in the roots.

—Rumi[1]

1. Rumi, quoted in Mamta Seghal, *Rooh-e-Rumi: Seeking God is Seeking Love* (India: Notion Press, 2019).

# Contents

꙳

# Foreword

Six weeks into the coronavirus pandemic, my family of six was sheltering in place in New York City. Schooling kids at home, trying to stay healthy, and maintaining a high workload, all underlaid by the uncertainty of what was coming next, was an overwhelming combination some days. One evening after the kids were in bed, I set down what I was working on, walked outside, and just looked up at the sky for five minutes. Nothing about my situation changed, but that tiny act of self-care in the form of pause shifted my perspective enough to carry on.

Life has one inevitable truth, right? Environmental chaos is a constant. In today's world, we are constantly bombarded with stimuli and choice, which can lead to decision fatigue and even paralysis. This type of cognitive overload can make even small tasks feel insurmountable (have you ever been so overwhelmed by life that the thought of folding that jeering pile of laundry seemed . . . impossible?). Fortunately, although we cannot prevent the chaos of the world, we can adapt ourselves to better cope with ever-changing circumstances, and through doing so bring about increased groundedness and fulfillment.

But attempting to revamp too much too quickly can be ineffective in the long run, even if it brings temporary relief. It is fighting fire with fire, chaos with chaos. Instead, we must ask ourselves: "What am I feeling? What are my needs? Are my existing habits allowing me to meet those needs?" Boiling down our thoughts, emotions, and behaviors to their most elemental form—to their roots—allows us to understand them, which is the first step to setting an intention for change. Simplifying that which feels so complex quiets the noise and puts you back in control.

As a clinical psychologist who is dedicated to helping people everywhere become healthier versions of themselves through behavior change, I wholeheartedly believe in the power of self-inquiry and exploration into one's personal motivations and core values. Breaking down deep-rooted, complicated behavioral inefficiencies into simpler, recognizable patterns is a technique I use every day in my practice. Through mindful reflection, we can begin to understand our fundamental needs and ultimate motivations (the "why" behind it all), and suddenly a path to changing and improving our daily habits becomes illuminated.

When Heidi Barr and Ellie Roscher approached me about penning this foreword, I was both personally humbled and professionally thrilled to see how brilliantly these behavioral constructs about which I am so passionate have been interwoven with fresh, exciting perspectives. I have had the pleasure of working alongside Heidi within the virtual walls of the behavior change company, Noom, for several years and am so pleased to see her areas of expertise collide in partnership with Ellie's in such a beautiful piece.

I have often found myself wondering how some people manage to harness and focus their energy in multiple directions with such grace, and now that I've read this book, I understand—Heidi and Ellie do so one tiny thing at a time.

I am delighted to introduce to you *12 Tiny Things: Simple Ways to Live a More Intentional Life*. It is a valuable resource for anyone and everyone, yet can be as uniquely yours as your life's journey. I hope it brings as much joy, understanding, and possibility to you as it has to me.

Dr. Andreas Michaelides,
Chief of Psychology at Noom, Inc.
April 2020
New York, New York

# Preface

The deep roots never doubt spring will come.
—MARTY RUBIN[1]

## Heidi

When we started developing a book that focuses on identifying the tiny things that help a person thrive and stay grounded, I had a stable, full-time job with great benefits. Life was good, things felt pretty easy most of the time, and adding a writing project to the mix was just the icing on the cake. Ellie and I started throwing ideas around, made an outline, had some meetings, and the project started to take shape. Then the bottom seemed to drop out of my life.

---

1. Marty Rubin, quoted in Melody Hamby Goss, *Poppies & Petals & Things That Fly* (United States: AuthorHouse, 2018).

After almost ten years at the same company, I was laid off unexpectedly. As my family's primary source of income, this was a major problem. At the same time, the issues of racism, climate change denial, misogyny, and homophobia were increasingly in the spotlight every day. It threw me off. My foundation felt cracked. I didn't have a job. The country was shifting. I wondered if I could write a book about tiny things. My life felt like too much of a mess to offer any sort of guidance. How could I muse over ideas and debate commas when I had to find new, affordable health insurance and decide whether to sell the house or not? It felt self-indulgent to spend time thinking about tiny things. There were bigger problems to solve in my own life, not to mention in the world at large. How could a few tiny things even matter?

Despite nagging doubts, I joined Ellie in practicing daily tiny things. And, as it turned out, focusing attention on tiny, but intentional, practices really helped me to weather the storm. These tiny practices became essential self-care. They were grounding. Exploring to the roots of things like home, food, and work helped me to process and claim what actually mattered.

Tiny things have become my cornerstone. They bring stability and peace. Finding the little practices that worked kept me rooted in the good stuff and moving in a direction that generates more life. Claiming, honing, and practicing what I value helped me stay true to what my soul was asking for. In a time of unease, I found it possible to stand, rooted in soul, and shining light into the world.

Regardless of how the ground feels underneath your feet, trust that there are roots there to tend. Deep in the earth, they know more life is on the way. They know spring will come, rising from the dirt, with all its color and vibrancy. By trying on one tiny thing at a time, you can slowly, deliberately and playfully, remember who you are. You can nourish that being with tenderness.

Together, we will reach and grow toward the sun.

# Introduction

... the most urgent question of the time: How much
is enough?

—WENDELL BERRY[1]

## Ellie

Several years ago, Heidi and I gathered a group of five women
over the same question: "What is enough?" We used the
Swedish word "lagom" as an anchor, which loosely translates
to "just the right amount." When I lived in New York City,
for example, not owning a car felt right. When I moved to
Minnesota and had a child, one car felt like enough. Susan,
one of the original five women and mother of two, also liked

1. Wendell Berry, *The Gift of Good Land: Further Essays Cultural and Agri-
cultural* (Berkeley: Counterpoint, 2018).

the life her family built around owning one car. "I like that sometimes we just have to say no to things," she explained. Meanwhile, Emily was trying to live locally for a year, not using a car at all. She had recently bought a home, with great intention placed on its location. She could walk to work, the grocery store, the library, and restaurants. Would her neighborhood be enough?

In our desire to be actualized and reflective people, we loved how agile and expansive the question felt. Clothes, self-esteem, technology, exercise, time—we applied the question to all the nooks and crannies of our lives. As women, as mothers, as humans living in a world full of stuff, in a world that links clutter to depression—especially in women—how much is enough? We chatted over coffee and tea. We started a blog. Five women grew to ten, varying and multiplying the conversation.

The world continued to shift in unpredictable ways, as it does, and more and more brokenness was spotlighted by the day—hunger, hatred, violence, fear, war, phobia. Everywhere you looked there was not enough. Not enough love, not enough food, not enough listening, not enough good education, not enough cooperation, not enough equity, not enough listening, not enough jobs or health care. It was overwhelming. In both of our personal and professional settings, Heidi and I started hearing the same thing over and over again: "I'm paralyzed. What do I do? Where do I start?"

I am a generalist with a bleeding heart. When I read the news headlines, an urgent and arrogant impulse rises up in me to alleviate the brokenness of racism and famine. I travel to Tijuana and want to fix the immigration crisis and erase sex slavery. I come home after working with teenagers wanting to address their mental health struggles and eating disorders with creative and compassionate solutions. The instinct to fix the world's problems comes from a place of deep compassion. Yet trying to work, write, parent, partner, contend with injustice, and reduce my carbon footprint all at once is neither strategic nor possible; it is also the quickest way to burnout. Instead of working effectively from a place of power, I haphazardly send my energy out in all directions. When I let the hurt seep in from all corners of the earth, I eventually find myself paralyzed and utterly ineffectual on the couch.

*12 Tiny Things* offers a place to start that is immediately available. It offers an alternative strategy for both the folks feeling stuck and the folks trying to solve the healthcare crisis before lunch. To tend to the global, we must also work on strengthening the hyper-local: the self. We can combat the instinct to be paralyzed by making assignments so laughably small that we cannot avoid them.

Not all people have the time, the resources, and the freedom to work on simplicity and intentionality. We imagine and work toward a world where all people have the leisure time and stability necessary to lead a reflective life, one of growth and self-actualization. There may be days, seasons, and stages where external circumstances make intentional living challenging. This book is about finding rootedness in life on the go. It celebrates that you do not need to extract yourself from your existing life to cultivate more alignment, presence, and satisfaction. Tiny things are available to us all. One tiny thing at a time, we can find ourselves thriving and more in love with our lives.

But these tiny things do not end with you, the reader. Improving ourselves can be a starting point, but it is not the ending point. This is a book about tending to our multi-faceted selves so that we may joyfully contribute to and nurture our communities. Improving the self will not auto-matically improve the world; yet, living from a place of evolv-ing inner peace and sense of wholeness will alter our work and relationships. Attention to the root system is part of the work, but not all of it.

This is a book about tiny things. Things that can go unnoticed in the everyday. Things that, to the stranger look-ing in, may seem inconsequential. Our culture tells us that bigger is better; more is always desirable. But when we go deep into the roots, we find that the tiny things make all the difference. They provide a foundation of beauty from which we can carve our own version of the good life. Our world tells us we are hungry while offering us empty calories to fill the void in the same breath. If we feed the tiny things that exist at our core, we will find nourishment. Nourishing our roots with intention gives life.

When imagining this project, an image of a tree kept coming up for Heidi and me. We realized practicing tiny things with intention felt like nurturing our roots. Identifying the tiny things became a journey underground to the invisible things that sustain us. There is great strength and wisdom in the foundation that often goes unseen. Aspen trees, for example, live in groves and share a root system. A grove is one life, one organism. Above ground it looks like a forest when indeed it is a single tree. A person may walk within a grove of aspen without knowing the intimate interconnectedness of the trees, without realizing that although the trees themselves are young, the grove may be thousands of years old and will likely last for several thousand more. Aspen survive the intense heat of forest fires and the severe cold of winter because of the deep life of the grove. The most permanent part of the tree, the roots can store information for long periods of time. Roots feel their way through the ground slowly, aware of stimuli, able to steer clear of toxic areas and find nourishment necessary for strength and growth. Trees embody the innate intelligence of the earth. They invite us to root so that we can rise.

In the ground beneath our feet, all of our roots are intertwined. When we tend to our individual selves, we strengthen us. This book, as well as the process of taking time on your own roots, is part of the conversation about enoughness. It is the work of shifting from a place of scarcity to one of abundance so our lives can be filled with joy, courage, and sustainable evolution as human beings.

*12 Tiny Things* is informed by the personal and professional lives of Heidi and me. We do not come to you as experts, but rather as co-travelers. Any time I caught myself hiding behind the role of author or facilitator, I felt depleted and wandering. Coming back to the practice of tiny things grounded me again. We invite you to join us, experimenting with work under the surface and continuing the conversation.

# Guidelines:
# How to Use This Book

Tiny things are different for all of us, but there are some common qualities. Even if your tiny things end up being different from what we suggest, these guidelines will help you navigate the process and uncover the practices that are right for you and your unique root system.

## Be gentle with yourself

This is hard, humbling work. Being kind and gentle with yourself is paramount. We believe that offering ourselves (and others) what Buddhists call "loving kindness" is essential for a healthy human life. Sometimes external circumstances make it difficult to stay calm. Life often throws turbulence just when we need gentleness. Sometimes our families challenge our desire to simplify and to be more intentional. Yet we can invite gentle energy in at any time. We can weave gentleness into the fabric of our days and let it inform our choices. We can honor ourselves and our experiences by being vulnerable and accepting support. We can honor everyone we encounter by showing up with full presence, listening with compassion, and offering encouragement instead of criticism. When you can be gentle with yourself and practice self-compassion, you are that much more likely to get to the root of what truly matters and figure out your tiny things.

## Be flexible

Finding, practicing, and integrating your tiny things is not for the faint of heart. It takes courage and honesty about what actually matters to you. And it takes a willingness to change your mind. Your tiny things may shift over time. What we value in our lives ebbs and flows over the course of a lifetime. Human life is not linear. It doesn't follow a straight path. Sometimes it jumps completely off the road and into a boat, or through a jungle of vines, or down the drain into the sewer. We have to be fluid and flexible with whatever direction life takes if we are going to stay true to this work. Some of your tiny things might stay the same forever. But some might change with the season, whether it be the season of the year or the season of life. We've found it's best to not hold on to any one thing too tightly. There is power in a gentle grip and a willingness to adjust.

## Name your inspiration

In the realm of behavior change, we know that figuring out what inspires action and drives choice is a key factor in sustainability. It's one thing to say, "I want to have more time for myself," and it's another to say, "I want to have more time for myself so I can feel refreshed and energized for each new day, showing up for my family as a whole, grounded person." Take some time to think about what draws you to this book and to the idea of making some changes to your life. What's under that desire for change? What's your "why"? Answering these questions moves us away from a deficit mindset, honors who we are, and helps us remember what is already inside us all. Tiny things are easy to pick up, but that also makes them easy to set down. Knowing our "why" helps us stay committed to the work when resistance shows up.

## Take small steps

Take small steps on the journey. Be kind, patient, and realistic with yourself. A majestic forest doesn't pop up overnight. Rome wasn't built in a day. Neither are intentional practices. For example, many folks take on the label of "too busy" because it is hard to say no to others. A first step could be simply noticing a time you say yes when you really wanted to say no. Then a few weeks later, you might pick a day of the week and guard it. Say no to every request for your free time on Wednesdays. Then a few weeks later you might practice saying no to something you don't want to do, even if you could logistically fit it into your schedule on a non-Wednesday. You worked up to it. Little steps are what get you moving in the direction you want to go. Little things are big things when you add a bit of patience and persistence.

## Embrace courage, not fearlessness

Being confident and owning your choices doesn't mean being fearless. In reality, no one is fearless. We all have the capacity to have courage and do things in spite of the fear that hovers overhead. You know the saying, "Feel the fear and do it anyway"? That's what living true to your roots requires. If you wait for fear to dissipate before you make the bold move (even if it's a tiny bold move) you'll never make the bold move. Desire authenticity and confidence more than the pull to stay safe. Strive for bravery over perfection. You just might feel more satisfied at the end of the day.

Choose to get to the root of the issue. Outsmart the fear.

## Own your discomfort

Feeling uncomfortable while making changes to habits and patterns is part of the deal—even though most of us don't care for that part of the process. The thing is, it's often that feeling of awkwardness or discomfort that propels you into new territory, a place where possibility is waiting. When you sit with the uncomfortable feelings that arise while experimenting with new ways of being, you are making progress. Make peace with the reality that you'll probably feel uncomfortable and awkward at least some of the time while trying out tiny things. You don't have to always live outside of that much-talked-about "comfort zone," but we all benefit from taking regular forays into uncharted (or forgotten) lands.

You can read this book front to back like a story, or you can start with the area that speaks most to what you need right now. There are twelve chapters, so you have the option to commit to this work for a year. Take a chapter a month and dig deep, reflect on that area of your life we discuss in each chapter, and try the tiny thing as part of your routine to see if you would like to integrate it into your life. Or not. Skip around. Take a week on one chapter and three months on the next. Invite a friend or group of people to do a tiny thing challenge with you. Journal about your practice. There are myriad ways to interact with the content. Maybe you'll love all the tiny things we suggest, and you'll try each one, one per month, for a whole year. Or maybe you'll find that just a few of our suggestions resonate, and you'll use the questions at the end of each chapter (and the appendix at the end of the book) to discern your own. You'll notice several "other voices," people in our lives who have shared which tiny things work for them in each area. Perhaps you'll take inspiration from their stories. With a bit of introspection, self-compassion, courage, and humor, we think you'll find the things you need to feel fully rooted in your life.

We each have a unique combination of small, intentional practices that fit and make a difference. There is no one-size-fits-all when it comes to what works. There is no silver bullet. Your experience of the world is as unique as your being. We invite you to use *12 Tiny Things* with playfulness and agility, trusting your instincts and ability to adapt what is presented here. Take what works for you and fly.

Name and claim the beauty in your days. Be present. Identify your desire. Practice mindfulness. Be creative. Find your tiny things and then use the power that comes from your newfound rootedness to impact the world for good. It's not about chasing happiness or climbing the ladder to what someone else has defined as success. It's about noticing, feeling, and claiming the things that will bring us contentment and satisfaction, and letting go of what doesn't. Consider the chapters that follow as an invitation to reignite your root system and claim your bliss.

# Space

\ˈspās\

*noun*

a continuous area or expanse that is free, available, or unoccupied

---

Saying no to one thing is saying yes to the possibility of another.

## Ellie

In 2007, a documentary about the Helvetica font was released, aptly titled *HELVETICA*. I recommended it to everyone I knew and often got skeptical looks in return. How could a film about a font be so interesting? Like any good documentary, it invites the viewer into a new world—in this case the world of typography, design, and our visual culture.

While delving into detail about how the font was created, Mike Parker, a distinguished type designer who helped popularize the font Helvetica, explains that the Swiss pay more attention to the background than the foreground in design. He maintains that negative space is what makes the font. Helvetica is pleasing to the eye because of the shapes that form from the unfilled space, the empty space within and between letters. It's as if the space holds the letters firmly in place, bringing stability and firmness. We tend to be so focused on what is right in front of us that we forget to look beyond, behind, and between. "[The letter] lives in a powerful matrix of surrounding space," he says. If you allow the background to become the focus, you begin to see the whole world differently, to appreciate the beauty of the space between.

When my yoga teacher calls me into Warrior 2 pose—which incorporates a wide leg base, a tall torso, an expansive, wide reach of the arms, and a turn of the head to look out over one extended arm—my teacher encourages me to set my gaze not on my fingertips or on the wall just beyond, but on the space between. Shifting focus, the room gets bigger. The world gets bigger. Once we see negative space, we can't unsee it, and we sense that there is room to dwell there. The space between is the connective tissue of the universe, reminding us that we are deeply connected to all creatures.

In the midst of a chaotic moment, we can stop and take a breath, creating space. There is space between where we are and where we want to go. In the in-between space, new things come into being.

### OTHER VOICES

When they need a little reboot, Suzanne's family declares a weekend day a Nothing Day. The whole family stays in their pajamas all day long and don't leave the house. It's against the rules to do work or hide behind screens. Their days are filled with reading, napping, cooking, eating, and playing games.

Some say music is the space between notes. Some say the space bar is the most important key on the computer because it gives meaning and rhythm to the other marks on the page. Notice the space between inhaling and exhaling. The margins of your book. The smooth tabletop. The space between you and the person nearby. The empty slot on your schedule. In the space between is potential, power, and peace. If we want more peace, we can broaden the space in our lives, reside in it, and appreciate it. We can invite the background to come into focus. There, we remember that we are not alone; we are living in a web of energy. The empty space holds us stable and firm.

As a wellness coach, Heidi helps clients see the space between. She told me about her client, Jan, who was working over fifty hours a week, managing her children's busy schedules, and tending to her mother, whom she had recently moved to an assisted living center. She also had multiple sclerosis and was required to meet with a wellness coach to keep her insurance premiums down. Instead of being excited to set health goals with a coach, she was reluctant to add one more thing to her list. It was the last thing she wanted to talk about. Because she was so overwhelmed, it felt like her world was spinning.

And yet, Jan attended those meetings despite a lengthy commute to work and long workdays. Her demanding boss made her feel bad about being overweight. Her siblings disapproved of their mother's move into assisted living. Her dog was sick. Her son wanted to paint his room orange. All of this was piling up. Frustrations arose from an inability to prioritize what really mattered most. There was not enough time in the day to do the things she really wanted to do.

Jan wanted more space, so that's where they started. Heidi invited her to put one hand on her stomach and take a breath. Together they inhaled for a count of three, paused, and let it out on a count of three. They repeated this several times. That moment of pause invited enough space to help Jan slow down and identify possibilities. Focusing on simply breathing fostered a sense of calm, a feeling of hope, and a willingness to work toward solutions. She said she'd try the intentional breaths again the next time her day felt like it was spiraling out of control.

### OTHER VOICES

Michelle overbooks her calendar with things that drain her. She bought a whiteboard calendar and named it her Wellness Calendar. She writes down things that give her life like dancing, coffee with a friend, naps, and lectures. She can see tangibly how well she is tending to herself. When she feels depleted, invariably circumstances have forced her to prioritize other things. Temporarily that's ok, but she works to get back to balance.

Sometimes space presents itself, other times we have to take a machete to our lives and fight for it with sweat and tears. We are often told that "more" is the solution. More work, more square footage, more gadgets, more money, more social events. We overfill our lives, hoping more will make us feel like we are enough. We focus on the letter instead of the space between. It takes courage to say no, but when we prioritize creating space, we can clearly see how saying *no* to some things is saying *yes* to others. We experience the inherent worth of the space itself. Carving out space in life is saying *yes* to our truest selves. Sometimes we are busy because we are vain. We want to appear important.

A crowded schedule helps us feel significant. Sometimes we are busy because it is easier. Instead of making hard decisions about priorities, we let others decide for us. Sometimes we are busy because we are scared of confronting our inner selves in the quiet moments. Yet doing more rarely works. If we can be brave enough to carve out space for ourselves, to dwell in the expanse, we can hear our most authentic selves calling us in the quiet.

### OTHER VOICES

When Julia and Kyle moved across the country, they purged most of their belongings. The space that remained felt inspiring, creative, and refreshing. Julia found more room in her mind for insight, wisdom, calm, joy, and love instead of clutter like worry and stress.

What would it look like to create more space in your life? Would you start with your closet, walls, inbox, or calendar? Your mind or Netflix queue? Your garage, basement, or social media profile? Can you pause long enough to let the background grow into the foreground? What grows will be even better than what you dare to imagine for your life. Perhaps the empty space will be exactly what you need.

Our lives are filled with figurative, literal, and digital clutter—a consequence of the quest for more. Clutter can make us feel constricted and anxious. Seemingly, the moment we are less diligent about removing clutter, it begins to accumulate again. We swoop through the house putting things back in place. We vacuum, dust, and reorganize. It often helps us feel better, and it always needs to be done again. There always seems to be something in a space we want empty.

There are days I feel like my full-time job has become picking things up. I pick up a coat from the floor and put it on the rack. I pick up bills from the counter, feathers that have escaped the couch, and Legos that are scattered throughout the house. I recently found the remains of a ham and cheese sandwich on the windowsill. Some evenings, I wonder if it makes a difference. I am the only one who seems to mind the clutter. On those evenings, I remind myself that tending to the clutter is for me. I am committed to managing the volume of stuff in my home. Decluttered areas help me stay calm, and the space created after decluttering leaves room for creativity.

Purging is a skill that we can hone as a first step to embracing space. We inherit our grandparents' knack for saving things just in case the next Great Depression waits around the corner. Yet our stuff weighs us down. Knowing that there are ties between clutter and depression, we can embrace mindful and incremental purging as a way of life. You'll be surprised what you don't miss.

Inner clutter isn't always as easy to identify as piles of accumulated stuff. Old negative thought patterns can take hold in our minds and redirect our entire day. Unchecked, our inner voice, telling us untruths, can increase in volume, and we start to believe the storylines.

Almost six months into being the primary caregiver to two children, I went to see my spiritual director because I was crying at work. While taking care of my two kids, I was trying to hold a part-time job and sneak in freelance writing and a book launch in the nooks and crannies of nap times and evenings. My work/life boundaries were muddy, and my professional to-do list dangled heavily over my head as I tried to stay present for my kids. Every free moment, I felt the obligation to chip away at writing. The cobbled-together time in the office for my part-time job was the only time away from my babies, so I felt vulnerable and exhausted. Transitioning from the energy and tasks at home to the energy and tasks at work was jarring, and I often got emotional. Although my work team was support-ive, it was getting ridiculous. Scheduling an appointment required finding a third babysitter to get through the day, but I decided it was time. My inner dialogue—the story I was telling myself—wasn't working.

At my spiritual director's office, I sat down, took a deep breath, and started with the emotions I was experi-encing around my milk supply being perpetually low. I felt betrayed by my body and was tired of working so hard to feed my baby. I knew the milk was just the beginning. My spiritual director and I unwound a metaphorical ball of yarn, airing out layers of emotion around the intensity of loving children. It became clear that I was operating out of a scarcity model. There wasn't enough milk, enough time, enough sleep, enough support. I wasn't enough. I was also equating showing my boys love with quantity of time together, regardless of how depleted I felt. My days lacked empty space.

### OTHER VOICES

With two active kids and an ambitious partner, Claire decided to try no-plans November. The family does not put social plans on the calendar for the whole month. This creates space for more family time and for spontaneous fun that would otherwise be scheduled away. The whole family looks forward to November to relax and see what unfolds.

My spiritual director said at one point, "What I just heard you say is that you need to put yourself away to take care of your boys."

"Yes," I said. That is how it felt sometimes. The self that likes to sleep uninterrupted, eat leisurely, read and write, see friends, and exercise had been dormant for a long time.

"Ok, well let's work on that. What would be a true statement you could use to replace that statement?" she asked.

"I honor myself and my boys when I am being my full self," I answered.

"Yes." Then she asked, "So, what would it take to wake up one morning feeling totally rested?"

I laughed and then realized she wanted an answer. I pretended to have no idea, but I knew exactly what it would take. It would take a bit more childcare during the day and some babysitting support at night so I could have more uninterrupted adult conversation. It would take a night away every now and again so I could have some alone time and sleep through the night. I knew all this, but I was simply afraid to claim it because I thought leaving my children meant I was a bad mom. In so many ways, it's easier to stuff parts of yourself away for later. Committing to the grind rather than letting space thrive and take up residence. The quiet that comes with space requires vulnerability and courage.

"You don't want to wait for your kids to be in school to grow into your whole self," my healer said. I wanted my boys to know my true-self and have that self as their primary caregiver.

By saying yes to the needs of my children exclusively, what needs of my own was I saying no to? Could I be brave enough to share my parenting role with other people now and again in order to tend to myself? With the help of a supportive community, I was able to let my needs breathe alongside the needs of my children, and I was able to shift from a model of scarcity to one of abundance. In the background space, I found potential, power, and peace. My healer helped me clear the clutter in my mind and start telling a true story about my reality. I was, indeed, enough.

This was good work for me, but I also wanted to model it for my children. When we overfill our schedules and our lives, we lower our opportunity for boredom. Research has shown that boredom is good for refreshing our brains, so we have to be brazen enough to tempt boredom. We can become dependent on external stimuli to keep us perpetually entertained. We can lean on others to give us a sense of identity. In the process, we forget how to sit with ourselves, be our own best friends, listen to the silence in our own being.

In mindful-based meditation, participants are taught to step outside continuous thoughts, to observe them without judgment. It's harder than it sounds, as anyone who has tried it knows. But when we can hear the stories we tell ourselves, we start to take control of the story. We become the author. We remember that we have the capacity to choose how we perceive what is happening in our lives. We claim the power that resides in that knowing. When we clear the internal and external clutter in our lives and let go of the messages and the stuff that are not serving us, we open ourselves up to personal transformation. The work creates a space that nurtures contentment. The balance we experience is true success.

The work of mindfulness demands constant diligence. It's so easy to slip back into the land of not-enoughness and reach for more as the answer. A balanced life is easy to talk about and much harder to build and claim. The centripetal force of society pulls us toward the foreground, where we locate the stuff, the busyness. In that place, though, I get depleted and lose my purest self. What is at stake is my energetic, silly, creative, calm, brave, curious, and open self. Crafting a life built on the importance of empty space is claiming a life that centers on joy, gratitude, self-care, acceptance, and empowered action. When I am acting from my healed self, I treat my calendar like a moral document and let it tell the truth about how I am spending my life. I keep space empty on my calendar. I put habits like running, yoga, writing, sitting, drawing, conversation, and meditation on my calendar. I take the time to ensure there's quietness, a time to dwell in the background space of my mind.

### OTHER VOICES

Christy is finding more space as a mom. She hands things over to her kids that she is in the habit of doing. She also marks space on her calendar when she doesn't plan anything for her kids or expect anything of them, so they can practice, too.

Now that women can do anything, we somehow own the sense that we have to do everything. We should do it all, have it all, be it all, and all at once. As gender roles become more dynamic, more pressure is put on men to do it all as well. But instead of being more, we can fade and disappear if we aren't careful. By subverting the pressure for more and denying the instinct to exist and take root in the foreground, we can reclaim the fertile, thriving garden of *enough* that lies at the heart of nothingness. There is an entire world, an entirely different way of being, in the space between. In quiet moments, we can see possibility. We can hear the pause between each breath and sense the peace it has to offer.

When I lean into the space of my life, I make smart purchases, and I don't let my house get cluttered with extraneous stuff. I sit still (almost) every day, gently allowing my breath to become a tool, and focus on things like calm, impermanence, letting go, being present, and gratitude. I run, breathing in the fresh air and letting my mind relax and reflect as my feet hit the pavement. When Heidi leans into the space of her life, I see her making better decisions about what work to take on, streamlining work, and creating small, achievable assignments so that work feels peaceful. We strive to create the space needed to feel rooted. We say no to invitations that don't serve us with confidence and clarity. We feel like human beings, able to just be and keep ourselves company. We wander and stray from this place of enoughness, of course, but it is where we strive to spend most of our time.

Back in Warrior 2 pose yet again, I gently set my gaze on the space between my fingertips and the wall beyond.

My teacher says, *"What you are looking for is looking for you."*
Through the sweat I smile, picturing my true self—a lighter,
calmer, more creative, and more joyful version of myself
working her way back home.

> ᠁ THE TINY THING ᠁
> ### An invitation to enough
>
> Another world is not only possible, she is on her way. On
> a quiet day, I can hear her breathing.
>
> —ARUNDHATI ROY[1]
>
> Say no to something. Maybe it's an item of clothing that
> doesn't make you feel good. Maybe it's a calendar item
> that you are dreading and don't need to attend. Maybe it's
> a thought in your mind that you know is not true. Notice
> the space that is created by saying no. Dwell in that space.
> See the potential, power, and peace there. Notice that
> lightning didn't strike you down. Find the courage to say
> no to something else, playfully acknowledge the space
> growing in your life.

---

1. Arundhati Roy, *War Talk* (Cambridge: South End Press, 2003).

## Body Practice

Once a day, intentionally look up. Don't just look up from your phone or your pile of work, look all the way up. Take in the vastness of the universe and feel the space holding you.

## In Reflection

* When was the last time you were bored?
* What would it require for you to wake up some day in the near future feeling rested?
* What would it mean to declutter your mind? Your closets? Your calendar? What would grow in the empty space?
* Take some time to really chart how you spend your time in a week. What do you notice?
* What in your life do you need to say no to? In saying no to that, what are you saying yes to?
* How does it feel to say no? Do you lie, make excuses, or over explain yourself? What would happen if you embraced *no* as a holy word and simply declined?
* What does your true Self look like?
* What is another tiny thing that could work to cultivate space in your life?

# Work

\ˈwərk\
*noun*

activity involving mental or physical effort done in order to achieve a purpose or result

mental or physical activity as a means of earning income; employment

Practicing presence is remembering how to live.

## Heidi

*"What do you want to be when you grow up?"*

What a loaded question to ask children. Often the translation is, "What paying job do you want to have as an adult?" We could ask, "Who do you want to be?" Yet those are not the words we use. Using *what* and *be* together implies our job is synonymous with who we are. It implies there is one answer and that there are acceptable and unacceptable ones.

My answer as a child was to be "a person who painted front doors yellow." That's it. Yellow made me feel happy and front doors were portals to love. The viability of door painting as a career path didn't cross my young mind. All that mattered was that painting was fun and front doors made me feel safe. All that mattered was that I liked how I felt when I imagined painting doors yellow.

Ellie told me that when she was little, she wanted to arrange bouquets of flowers for her job. She liked the thought of being surrounded by vibrant colors and smells and the idea of building arrangements that would make others happy. When her mom told her it wouldn't make enough money, she was devastated. She then went searching for a job that adds beauty, makes others happy, and supports herself. Eventually her answer became doctor. It fit the criteria, and she got positive reinforcement for that answer, so it stuck. It took her years to decide that it wasn't actually what she wanted to do.

*What do you want to be when you grow up?*

What better, open, and curious questions can we ask children as they dream and grow and unfold? Lately, when

I ask my daughter what she wants to be when she grows up, she says, "I want to help animals as a vet. And have fun painting. Also write books and be a gymnast." Once I changed the question to "*Who* do you want to be when you grow up?" She looked at me askance and said, "I want to be me." Her dreams are still unfolding, but she knows what she wants—to be herself. Her dreams are about what lights up her eyes. They aren't about a specific paying job or career path. What matters to her is being present in her life right now.

---

**OTHER VOICES**

Jerome and Sarah quit their jobs and moved from Minnesota to Utah. For them, work is a means to earn income while allowing ample time off to do what they love. Their meaning comes from something bigger than what they do for pay. Jerome and Sarah come alive carving through fresh powder under a bluebird sky. They are working to live, not living to work.

---

As adults, instead of asking "*Who are you?*" or "*What are your passions?*" or "*What gives your life meaning?*" We ask each other, "*What do you do?*" The question still implies one unchanging answer and equates our jobs—what we get paid to do—with our worth. We want our work to matter. We want to matter. Yet, our work is more varied than our jobs, and our being is more varied than our work. We are not what we have. We are not what others think about us. We are not what we do. We are ourselves, and how we show up to whatever we do in life is what matters.

I changed majors five times in college. From English to art to anthropology to psychology, I eventually took my mother's advice and picked health. After a few stints at health clubs as a personal trainer post-graduation, I took a job as a telephonic health coach. I called people on the phone, asked them questions about motivation, encouraged them to adopt healthier habits, and facilitated the formation of a plan toward success. I helped them track their goals, and they shared their progress with me on a website. As a remote employee, all work was done in front of a computer screen. Messages, emails, phone calls. Messages, emails, phone calls. Sometimes I felt like a robot. After ten years of the same routine, it felt tedious and draining, despite the knowledge that my work was helping people lead healthier lives.

"How we spend our days is, of course, how we spend our lives,"[1] Annie Dillard reminds us. If we think of work in terms of tasks, I spent my days (and thus my life) sending emails and scrolling websites while sitting at a desk. That's not how I wanted to spend my life. What I truly wanted was to spend time roaming woodland glades or watching

---

1. Annie Dillard, *The Writing Life* (New York: Harper & Row, 1989).

sunlight dapple my daughter's laughing cheeks. I was fully invested in my identity as "health coach," yet it was quite easy to feel dissatisfied with work when I focused on the daily messages, phone calls, and emails, or when I dreamily thought about what I would rather be doing.

What if we change the question? What if, with everyone from small children to grown adults, we focused on the *who* and the *how* of our work instead of the *what*?

*How are you showing up to the daily task list? Where do you put your energy?*

I started thinking about who was on the receiving end of my emails. Was I rushing through the process, trying to do three other tasks at the same time, or did I put the whole of my focus on the words going out into the universe? I became mindful of my posture: was I slouched forward, shoulders around my ears, or was I aware of how the chair felt against my spine, shoulders back and down? I thought about what I was allowing the computer to take hold of— was I scrolling through acres of needless information, or was I being intentional about using technology as a tool?

Presence can be the most rewarding part of our daily practice. When we can remember that, then whatever the task list, we're more able to find satisfaction in how we spend our days, and ultimately, our lives. There is joy in recognizing that life is more than what we see, or even what we do, on the surface. It is how we are showing up that matters at the end of the day.

One crisp autumn morning, I woke to the sun rising through a pink haze of clouds floating above an utterly still lake. Outside I could see my breath. The grass by the lake was sparkling with frost. As the sun gathered strength, I looked toward the western sky to appreciate the deep blue transition from night to dawn. I stood on the dock and watched a duck glide through misty waters. It was stunning, and I felt every nuance of aliveness coursing through my veins.

I realized then how often the beginnings of my days were being lived out in front of a screen. Giving those first waking moments away to technology made me apt to miss the gift of witnessing a new day coming into being. I missed seeing my breath melt into the breath of the earth, and I didn't notice the other forms of life that add depth and diversity to my human experience.

Screens and task lists and job titles have value. The answer is not throwing our devices in the lake and quitting our jobs. Yet beginning the day (no matter what work is on the task list) in the analog rather than virtual world has a positive impact. When I began starting my day with ten to twenty minutes outside, or at least away from a screen, I felt grounded in a tangible reality that I could touch, smell, and taste. This helped me show up to work in a more genuine, less robotic, way. Starting my workday by walking outside to see the last of the stars fade into the dawn, taking a moment to feel the moss on the north side of the trees, marveling at the different ways life finds to express itself, all made a difference. It allowed me to let all feelings—even the unwanted ones—present themselves. It invited me to speak and move into each day rooted instead of frazzled. It helped me face the work tasks I'd rather avoid. Ensuring my mornings started with wild air, fading starlight, and the peace that keeps company with wild things became as essential as any other task on the list. Practicing presence made work more meaningful and enjoyable. It kept me going on days when work threatened to be just another four-letter word.

### OTHER VOICES

As a life coach, Leslie has put in her fair share of hours listening with her head and heart. A common struggle she sees with folks is that they are not speaking their truth. They diminish their true feelings in order to be liked or to remain feeling safe at work. She helps people get to the heart of the issue and find accurate words to use at work to communicate clearly. To find liberation at work, many people need to speak up.

We are living in a season that requires presence. The boundaries between work and home are dissolving. Gender roles are blurring. A changing job market calls for changing jobs. More folks are working from home. Presence in work life means, in part, being present to each stage of life, which requires agility. We can weave together a meaningful life that has meaningful work as part of it. We take turns with our partners, move cities, and shift markets. Sometimes work feels like work, like a job, what we get paid to do. Sometimes it feels like a holistic vocation. Sometimes it is a dream come true where everything is inline and balanced. Sometimes not. It always means that who we are, the person we bring to the moment, is more important than what we do. When fully present, when willing to shift with the tide, we can find that each stage has something new to offer.

Being present means paying attention to invitations. *Do what you love and then figure out how to get paid for it*, or so the saying goes. Ellie shared with me that as a teenager, she was the pitcher on the varsity softball team. Toward the end of high school, she got a call from a man she had never met before. He asked if she would be interested in teaching his daughter how to pitch.

"I'll pay you $20 a lesson," he said.

Her mouth fell open for a moment. That was a lot of money. "Yes," she answered. "I'd love that."

And she did. She loved sitting on a bucket in the sun, spending time with great athletes, figuring out drills and progressions. She never would've come up with the idea on her own or been brave enough to charge $20 per lesson. She liked the work so much that within a year she was giving five lessons a morning all summer long. At a pivotal time, she learned what it felt like to get paid to do something she loved.

Living in the here and now means knowing when to be brave enough to pivot, being open to the possibility that a new life stage is beginning that might require a different way to work. There was a moment in college when Ellie realized that her life was actually *her* life. She was in a four-hour chemistry lab. Each week she dreaded it beforehand, despised it during, and begrudged it afterward. It dawned on her that she had registered for the class. No one forced her to become a pre-med student. Just because she could pass the classes didn't mean she had to. Feeling like she should be a doctor wasn't enough. She didn't want to be stressed out for a decade preparing to be a doctor, so she didn't. She committed to being present to what sounded fun, what woke up her being. She spent her time doing things that helped her be an actualized version of herself.

Later, Ellie adored her work as a high school teacher and coach. Like in my work as a health coach, it required a lot of relational energy to do well. The harder she worked, the more results she got with young people. The more energy I put into health coaching conversations, the more I felt like I was helping. The more we both did in our respective roles, the more we were rewarded. Ellie and I both really wanted our work to matter, and these jobs fed that desire. It was fulfilling.

Yet it was so easy to work to exhaustion and crash out every day off. Ellie was *so* present to her work during those teaching years that she didn't have anything left for the rest of life. I was *so* intent on being a high performing health coach that the more good reviews I received, the more I struggled with compassion fatigue and burnout. As the years passed, it became clear to Ellie that she was giving her best self to her job while the other areas suffered. It became necessary to diversify to include more time for other things. She transferred what she loved most about teaching to another job that supported a more balanced way of living. She realized that she's a generalist, someone who's happy doing many different things, not a specialist. I realized that being my best overall self meant giving less to work, even if it meant I was no longer the top performer in the department.

For some folks, *"What do you do?"* may never have a simple answer, and that's fine. It requires staying agile and being brave enough to fully engage in the here and now. As lives evolve, paid jobs simply became one puzzle piece in the big picture. Ellie and I both crave a life sustainable enough that it doesn't need an escape plan. Figuring out what needs to change to allow being our full selves, not just what we're paid to do, is always a good pivot.

Sometimes, however, we are not in control of our pivots. In the midst of honing my practice of being present at work, my boss told me that my position had been eliminated. After a decade working at the same company, suddenly I didn't anymore. It felt like someone had pulled the rug out from under me, leaving me lying on the floor, staring at the ceiling, wondering what happened. I had felt effective at my job for nearly ten years. For the most part, I liked what I did, and I felt like my work mattered. It allowed me the lifestyle I wanted.

Without that job, the threads that held my days together felt tenuous. It was unnerving. I felt raw and bitter, like an empty shell of myself. After all that time spent figuring out how to be more present, I didn't want to be present to this. Being numb or distracted seemed like better options.

In mainstream America, work has a tendency to be a defining feature of how we identify ourselves and how we measure our worth and value to the world. It's a key ingredient for how we tend to find meaning in our lives. Being successful at work, for better or worse, matters in our culture. And when work as we know it goes away, it's disorienting, even for those of us who think we know how to look deeper than a job to find life's purpose. Without a job, I felt unmoored. I wanted to locate meaning for myself outside of my profession and be totally present to life without work, but it was hard. When asked, "*What do you do?*" I didn't know what to say. I had to lean into a pivot I didn't want.

In the space created by that pivot, I found a small sense of relief that I had to try something new after years of doing the same thing. Yet, I was also terrified. What if I couldn't do anything else? What if I was ousted as a fraud, as someone who isn't actually a valuable asset to any organization— a failed experiment? Not successful? After all these years trying to find life's meaning in a job, what if without a job there was indeed nothing left? I tried to remind myself that there was still meaning in my life and that life was more than a job. This was easier said than done.

I started asking myself, "Where do I find meaning?" It took a while to quiet the self-doubt, but when I really listened, the answers came. Meaning started showing up in holding space for people, in listening, in offering support, in bearing witness to challenge. Meaning showed up in pulling carrots, in kneading bread, in feeding people, in dipping a canoe paddle into the lake. Meaning showed up in the sunrise, in the caress of the wind, in planting seeds, in the laughter of children. I found meaning in being present to the details.

Many of these meaning-makers made an appearance in my job over the years. As a wellness coach, I listened to people all day long and helped a lot of folks figure out how to take care of themselves. I spent time in silence with those who were struggling. I encouraged people to get outside and to cook more at home. Yet when this work went away, all of that meaning remained. It was still there in planting seeds in the garden, or in listening to a neighbor's story, or cooking a healthy meal, or sharing the harvest.

I experienced feelings of anxiety, disappointment, and bitterness when I was laid off. Mixed in was curiosity, relief, and anticipation of what might be next. I remembered that any job is simply one slice of life and being present in it all is possible.

I continued to start my days with non-virtual time even when my job ended. It was still just as essential. Avoiding immediately jumping into the digital fray of job hunting or social media helped me remember what brings true meaning to my day-to-day. I wanted to embrace the world in a way that made me feel alive. I wanted to prioritize the things that felt meaningful, the things that invited presence. I wanted to show up in my days rooted, to cultivate a life of purpose and beauty.

One morning a few months into being unemployed, I rolled out of bed feeling a little annoyed with myself. I hadn't been getting up in a very timely manner. The lack of routine had disrupted my balance. That unmoored feeling was proving hard to shake. I felt like I'd forgotten some aspects of how to live as a modern, gainfully employed human.

I padded into the kitchen to feed the cats and switch on the coffee maker. The back-deck thermometer read minus-nine, but the sun was shining and there was no wind. I was craving some fresh air, so I pulled on some fleece-lined long underwear, a hat, and a facemask. If the snow is just right—not too much, packed down, no big bare ice patches—it's possible to skate ski around the lake's perimeter. I grabbed my skis and headed outside. Unmoored or not, I could still ski.

Down at the lake, I clipped into my skis and pushed off. The ice creaked and groaned as I glided across the frozen white expanse. The wind was bitter, but my body was warm.

With my face turned toward the sun, I took a deep breath. My lungs appreciated the fresh air despite its frigidity.

The sky was vivid blue, the air vibrant. Time seemed to stand still even as the dock appeared again. I finished a loop and sat down on the dock to adjust one of my ski boots. In the stillness of the cold air, I looked up and saw a gray fox's tail disappear into the forest through a shimmer of frozen sunshine. In that moment, I remembered that I know how to live, no matter what "work" means. I remembered that what I want in my life is to be present to the beauty that exists when I make a point to notice it. Paying job not required.

### ᵐᵂᵗ THE TINY THING ᵗᵂᵗ
#### An invitation to presence

Let the beauty of what we love be what we do.

–RUMI[2]

Spend the first minutes of your day in the analog world. Even five minutes can make a difference if you are used to opening your eyes and checking email on your phone while still in bed. (To set yourself up for success, put your

2. Coleman Barks. *The Essential Rumi* (New York: Castle Books, 1995).

screens away the night before, ideally out of the bed-room. Get an old school alarm clock if necessary.) No matter the duration of your non-virtual time, start the day engaging with something that doesn't have a screen, perhaps not even a plug. Enjoy being present instead of distracted by whatever wants your attention via email or social media or the Outlook calendar. Be where you are physically located, and only there. Watch the sun greet the day, and really notice how it lights up the sky. Step outside to check the weather. Drink your coffee and only drink your coffee. Starting the day in grounded simplic-ity allows us to navigate whatever the day brings, whether it be virtual chaos, a traffic jam, or back-to-back parent-teacher conferences.

Start your day in the here and now. Because being present for life is the only way to be fully alive.

## Body Practice

At some point in your workday, make your neck long, and roll your shoulder blades down your back, toward your spine so your heart shines out to the world. Let it be a reminder to bring your full presence—who you are—to all you do.

## In Reflection

* What does work mean to you?
* Visualize a great day doing your typical day-to-day work. What makes it feel good? What gives it meaning and purpose?
* How do you tend to "show up" in your workday?
* What makes you feel satisfied with your day-to-day?
* How do you stay present at work? What helps you focus on one thing at a time?
* What would be different if you felt present and rooted in the here and now, no matter what was on your task list?
* What reminds you that you are alive?
* What is another tiny thing that could work to cultivate presence at work?

# Spirituality

\ˈspiriCHoo͞ˈaləde̅\
*noun*

the quality of being concerned with the human spirit
or soul as opposed to material or physical things

Tend to the things you want to grow.

### Ellie

On a summer day, Montefiore Square was full of people
playing dominoes and doing Tai Chi. They were moving
slowly, intentionally together. It was a beautiful communal,
public practice. In the middle of the park, an old man was

doing temporary calligraphy. Bright white hair poked out from underneath his dark baseball hat. He wet a long paint-brush with water from a bucket, hunched over slightly, and wet the pavement with beautiful writing. Every few characters he paused, referring to a poem he was holding in his left hand. He repeated the same lines over and over and over again. Slowly, mindfully. Dip, stroke, stroke, stroke, dip. His writing hand moved like he was conducting an orchestra in an underground pit. I looked out across the pavement with fresh eyes and saw years of art, layers of words encased there, whispering to us about life and death and love and heartache. The poem waited briefly to be discovered before the graceful symbols evaporated in the afternoon sun.

The fleetingness of the water, the sacred detachment of his practice had something to teach me. I knew it in my bones. He was mesmerizing, dipping and stroking as if he had all the time in the world.

What a curious man. Why this poem, this practice? Was it penance? Obsession? Devotion? Maybe it was a love poem he was sending out to the one he lost, adding layers of sorrow and grief to the ground. Or maybe he simply believed in the art of repetition, the pure goodness of beauty and the fleeting nature of things.

The fading symbols invited my mind to wander to my spouse's kisses—generous beyond counting—stroking my lips, cheeks, hands, and neck over and over again. Gentle art, wet poetry, evaporating. Layers of love becoming part of my body's story. Small moments of beauty encircling me on a journey.

His practice seemed like a spiritual discipline, like returning to my yoga mat or prayer cushion day after day to practice, to see what is mine to learn in a new moment, as a new self. There is nothing to count. Every day there is something simple and profound in the practice, a journey to seek truth in me and around me. In corpse pose, or deep in meditation, I detach and let it go. I move on, sweat evaporating, glistening with newness.

There is no keeping score.

### OTHER VOICES

Inspired by the prayer life of her Muslim friends, Patricia set a mobile phone alarm to chime each hour from 9:30 am to 9:30 pm. When she hears the sound, she takes a deep breath and turns inward for a few moments. This small pause helps her remember what she values.

Watching this man practice, I thought of my dedication to studying theology and writing, not for recognition but because of my deep love of it, and the inherent value of the process. I thought of the hours I've spent poring over books, seeking insight and light. I thought of taking a moment to close my eyes and swim through my mind for just the right word to capture a feeling of an idea. Attaching an effective word to an ethereal idea or studying the work of great minds before us feels like chasing evaporating water, like luring a transcendent idea to become imminent and dwell among us. The process of seeking knowledge and wisdom often feels like chasing evaporating water, yet there is goodness in the pursuit of truth. The rigor is intoxicating.

Watching the Chinese characters, I hoped they would stay a bit longer. I didn't want this moment to fade, but it did.

"*Using water feels like a waste of time,*" my fears whispered to me. I reach for ink, permanent marker and oil paint instead of water. I rush to type and post my own words instead of reflecting on the wisdom of another. I am driven to make a mark, to be recognized for excellence. I want it to count. I want to count. I want to be immortal, to stick, to go on. Fearing mediocrity, my ego strives for more public accolades in order to accumulate happiness and peace.

We are sold the lie that we will get there. There is a destination. We can earn it; we are entitled to it. In an unending quest, there is no room for quiet devotion, for vulnerable dependence, for committed practice, for the mundane. When we get there, we will plant a flag and then we will matter. We will conquer. We will be whole and happy. Life will be easy. We will have arrived.

And practicing dissolving poetry in the park will not get us there.

The truth is, there is no destination or arrival. I am not what I produce. Life is not a competition. I am an unfolding creature held in the holiness of life. I simply have to choose to pay attention to the evaporated art under my feet. I pause under the warm shower water and breathe in the morning. I sip coffee, smelling the bitter aroma and feeling the liquid coat my stomach. I sit in traffic and stand in line with intention. I chop sweet potatoes and dice garlic with a smile on my face. I dry dishes, watching the soap suds disappear into the embroidered rag with gratitude. I place the square, white dishes back in the cupboard for tomorrow. I give caressing kisses first thing in the morning, in the middle of play, at nap time, while reading books, when helping on and off the highchair, car seat, and toilet, and again at bedtime, all while feeling fully alive. I fold blue towels, superhero underwear, green sheets, and dinosaur T-shirts affectionately. Repeat. This is it.

I could go to the park today with a poem and a brush. I choose to think, to stay alive, to treat others with compassion. I can practice being human in all its messiness and mortality and decide what has meaning. I can decide what to worship. I can choose to fold laundry and sip coffee and kiss babies and find dignity in devotion and dependence. I can proclaim, "This is life!" I am arriving every fleeting moment. Hidden in plain sight before me is something on fire with sacredness. There is poetry trapped on the carpet at my feet. There is ancient art evaporating all around me.

Spirituality is in the noticing. Attention to earth, fire, wind, water, space. Attention to the connection we feel to the earth and other creatures. When we feel adrift, it's an invitation back to attention, back to devotion. It's an invitation to light a candle and watch the flame, to step back on the yoga mat for five or ten or forty-five minutes, to stretch a tight muscle, or to reach out to a friend.

## OTHER VOICES

Two years after a hurtful divorce, Kathryn was still consumed by anger and resentment. She had done amazing work, and was ready to be on the other side of something. She designed an ending ritual and invited her ex-husband. She asked for forgiveness and forgave him. They lit things on fire, said prayers, and sang in front of a few witnesses. It did indeed bring closure and a chance for pivot into something new.

*Spirituality* can be a trigger word for people. It's a loaded term in part because of its tie to religion. "I'm spiritual, not religious," is a popular distinction, a stance to distance ourselves from the historical missteps, the potential narrow-mindedness and the rules and dogma of organized religion. By dropping religion, however, we often drop the ritual and practice that recognizes the sacred in the mundane moments of life along with it. If we are spiritual beings, where do we shift our attention? What practice brings us back to what matters?

The old Chinese man painting poetry with water in the park was immersed in a practice, a ritual that invites us to acknowledge and pay tribute to the beauty all around us. In his movements, he gently pointed to the truth that transcends time and place.

It takes time to say the things that need to be said, and ritual can help us speak. Ritual makes tangible the intangible. It incorporates the body and the being, infusing the extraordinary in the most ordinary objects. It validates and celebrates turning points in the human experience. It breathes life into the monotony of our days.

How we spend our days is how we spend our lives. If we walk away from ritual and practice, we limit our experience of the world as conscious beings. In this way, I tend to think the other chapters in this book are as much—if not more—about spirituality than this one.

There is art in repetition—a rhythm to returning to a ritual or practice again and again. This is also something religion can do as well. Muslims pray five times daily. Jews practice a weekly day of rest. Christians enter into a time of contemplative waiting during Advent annually. It is important to circle back to themes and deepen our being instead of always trying something new. When my first child was three, he realized seasons repeat. He got so excited thinking that it will get warm and we can go swimming again! We can go to the apple orchard again next fall. He will have another birthday! We yearn for cycles, for repetition, for seasons, for another try.

## OTHER VOICES

Megan is a pediatrician who specializes in palliative care. That means, essentially, she helps children die well. In her time off, she started knitting warm, beautiful sweaters for all the babies being born in her life. The spiritual practice helps her be still and rest, and creating something tangible sooths her mind. She wants to celebrate the healthy children in her life, too. Knitting brings her balance and hope, one stitch at a time. It helps her show back up at work to sit with people in their sorrow.

Whether your practice is doing yoga, picking up rocks on walks, reading ancient texts, singing, meandering through the woods, mindfully drinking your coffee, meditating, lighting candles, keeping a gratitude journal, acknowledging the energy in the soil as you garden, or washing dishes at attention, that practice can become a spiritual one with simple intention and mindfulness. A life-affirming ritual can come from any transformative practice. Embracing the art of repetition and thus building spirituality into our days adds depth and breadth to our ordinary lives.

It is worth noting that the man painting poetry was not the only one in the park. There were also people playing dominoes and doing Tai Chi. Ritual and practice can add depth when done in community, with witnesses and with accountability moving toward collective truth.

Spirituality is in the placing of ourselves in an interdependent web of life. It's an acknowledgement that we are not the center of the universe. It orients us as small and insignificant in the expansive universe and the unfolding history, while honoring our unique individuality and power in this very time and space. There is a centripetal force pulling us toward the status quo of greed in our society, and it can be toxic for us and our neighbors. Choosing a counter energy can place us in a space where the common good is nurtured and we feel connected to ourselves, each other, the earth, and all creatures. Spirituality is the lens we choose to use to see the world. When I use a lens of abundance, I tend to be a happier, more generous person. My life feels meaningful and full.

Heidi once told me about her home yoga space. On a shelf next to a candle, she keeps a rock that she picked up on the shores of Malta twenty years ago. This type of rock is known to some as a goddess stone. It is peppered with little holes because it has been tossed around and beaten up, made smooth, and cracked open again. Its journey from the sea to land has left marks. It's said that they always wash up where they are supposed to, more beautiful, more filled with life, and lighter than before. Their holes give them room to grow. Their holes give them the space they need to evolve and remember the wholeness that they have always had.

Heidi likes turning her goddess stone over in her hand, feeling the bumpy surface and rough grooves. As she stands there, rock in hand, in her basement, she remembers the rocky beach where she picked it up years before, and a sense of connection washes over her. Touching this rock transports her to a place across the world, reminding her that somehow she *is* this rock, that beach, and that sea, even while she is this body, this mind, this person. She remembers there is something sacred here in this simple ritual of touch.

When Heidi holds the rock between her hands, she can feel the solid nature of earth and the beauty of imperfection that it represents. That same energy runs through every human being. We don't live in a perfect world. Our journeys make their marks on our bodies. We are full of holes.

Cultivating a spiritual practice, even something as simple as holding a rock or taking an intentional breath, helps us embrace our imperfections and stay awake for the ride. Some days it is painful, and we skip it. We get so sucked into the task at hand or the stress of the week or the anxiety of the situation, that we forget we're breathing. We forget we're connected to the life force that is always there, grounding us. Sometimes weeks, or even years go by when we let things distract us, and we find that we've floated away from any sort of practice. Sometimes we feel adrift, but even when we do, our breath is always there. Our practice is waiting. When we return, when we give attention to the things that help us see the sacred in the ordinary, the sacred in the land base, the sacred in the community, the sacred that courses through our own bodies, we find the kind of devotion that connects life to the divine. Spiritual practice is feeling grounded in reality and connected to the vastness beyond human life in the same breath.

## OTHER VOICES

Part of Michelle's spiritual practice is honoring her own story. She has a small altar in her room with objects that represent important people, moments and ideas that have shaped who she is becoming. By knowing herself and her story, she believes she can better access the universe.

Practicing spirituality, honoring our whole beings, can bring us back to truths that we have strayed from, including the truth of who we are at our most authentic selves. It is a space where we can ask big questions and experience great suffering and great joy with our neighbors. It calls us to a reflective life, one filled with wonder and awe and ceremonies of the everyday. It can get us simultaneously into ourselves and out of ourselves. Reaching and grounding. Striving and resting. Like our very breath.

---

ᵐᵞᵖᵀ   **THE TINY THING**   ᵗᵞᵉᵗ

### An invitation to attention

Attention is the beginning of devotion.

—Mary Oliver[1]

Choose a comfortable position in a quiet place. Take three breaths, slightly slower and fuller than usual. For those three inhales and exhales, become aware of your breath. Allow the sound and the rhythm of your breath to soothe you. On your inhales, reach the crown of your head toward the ceiling. On your exhales, ground into the earth through the bottom of your feet. On your inhales, accept new life, new energy, new opportunity into your tense muscles. On your exhales, let go of something you are clinging to that is not serving you. Pull deeper inside

---

1. Mary Oliver, *Upstream: Select Essays* (New York: Penguin Press, 2016).

of yourself and listen to your truth. Gently blink your eyes back open.

Your breath is always with you. It is a built-in calming tool. It reminds us that we are alive. We are here now. Recognizing yourself helps you recognize the universe. Over time, your three conscious breaths can become four, five, six and so on. Try square breathing, where you inhale for four counts, hold for four counts, exhale for four counts, and hold for four counts. Try different body positions while breathing—standing at attention, laying like a corpse, sitting straight on a chair, or curled in the fetal position. It will help you stay awake and attuned to your unfolding self in this one glorious life.

## Body Practice

Once a day, pick your toes up and place them back on the ground intentionally. Splay them out wide and feel your strong foundation. Notice your connection to the plot of ground on which you stand. Be where you are. Let your attention lead you toward devotion.

## In Reflection

* What does the word *spirituality* trigger in you?
* What do you feel devoted to right now?
* Can you bring mindfulness to part of your daily practice so it becomes ritual?
* In what areas of your life do you catch yourself keeping score?
* When have you successfully let go and let things dissolve?
* What happens in your body when your breath becomes slower and fuller? What happens to your mind? What calls your attention? How do you feel after you opened your eyes?
* What are you doing, who are you with, where are you when you feel most connected to yourself, to others and to the earth? How can you incorporate this awareness into your daily life?
* What is another tiny thing that could work to cultivate attention in your life?

# Food

\fo͞od\

*noun*

any nutritious substance that people or animals eat or drink, or that plants absorb, in order to maintain life and growth

Breaking bread mindfully is everyday alchemy.

## Heidi

I come from a family of farmers, which is something I didn't always appreciate growing up, but for which I am deeply grateful now. As a child, I learned firsthand where food comes from. My parents grew their own vegetables, and I have many (albeit not always fond) memories of dripping yogurt cloths and mysterious jars of sprouts in dark cabinets. Dad baked bread regularly. The pressure cooker hissed every August when my mom canned beets. Shelling peas and taking out the compost were part of the routine. Being that close to the origin of my food allowed me to witness the everyday alchemy of how simple ingredients and practices, when combined just right, are transformed into life-giving nourishment.

I took ownership of my own bread making when I was living in a valley nestled between the Red Cloud and Sawtooth Mountains in Idaho. Two summers spent as an assistant cook at a youth wilderness camp, plus twice weekly bread-baking sessions, provided ample opportunity to practice combining water, yeast, flour, oil, honey, molasses, and a bit of salt. I learned how to knead the dough smooth and when to punch it down again. I learned how to form the dough into uniform loaves and how to tell when to take them out of the oven. I also happened to learn how to carry fifty-pound sacks of whole wheat flour down a narrow staircase and how to keep mice from getting into the storage room. We used a bread recipe that made seven loaves at a time, and I eventually became pretty capable of turning out something edible for the camp guests. There's not much better than homemade bread after spending all day on a mountain trail. All of that kneading strengthened my forearms and being able to provide comfort and energy for others felt a little like magic.

### OTHER VOICES

Jacob and Andrew's organic vegetable farm provides restaurants with locally grown produce. In the summer, they work fifteen-hour days cultivating, weeding, harvesting, washing, packing, and delivering the goods. Once a day they stop, sit down, and enjoy a meal straight from the soil. They eat what they grow. The fruits of their labor nourish thousands.

After those summers of baking bread every day for three months straight, you'd think I would have continued the practice. But I didn't. Instead I went back to college after each summer, and baking fell promptly off the radar in the wake of studying, local pubs, and life in a dorm room.

It wasn't until well after college that I decided to throw some water, yeast, flour, oil, honey, molasses, and a bit of salt into a bowl together again. After mixing up some dough using fragmented memories of that old camp recipe, I kneaded, let the dough rise, punched it down, and formed loaves. I put them in the oven and waited in anticipation for them to be done. They smelled wonderful. The timer went off, and I gleefully cut into one with a serrated knife. Rather, I tried to cut into one. They were rock hard, suitable for holding the door open in the summer. Heavenly-smelling paperweights.

A few weeks later I tried again, this time with a printed recipe and fresh ingredients. The result was better, but not good. I made it through a few slices before chucking it out to the squirrels. I kept returning to the practice of mixing flour, water, yeast, honey, oil, molasses, and a bit of salt until I didn't need to follow the recipe point by point anymore, until I could feel the dough coming into a smooth, desirable consistency. The results of my practice became shareable. I have been making a loaf or two a month ever since.

There are rules to follow, but intuition and feel are involved. Mostly I use no-fuss recipes, but every once in a while, I'll try an intricate scaling technique. Some recipes require lots of kneading. Some require none. No matter what technique is used, the bread that comes into being is well worth the effort. Kneading, the combination of hands in dough, works out the kinks of the day. Waiting for bread to rise offers reason to pause. The yeast or sourdough starter do their magic and take on a life and story of their own. The alchemy of simple, cheap ingredients coming together to nourish the soul and the body is as elemental as it is profound.

Baking bread invites me to slow down, to savor the entire process of creating something from simple ingredients. When I bake bread regularly, I am more in tune with the part of myself that has the capacity to use my choices in a way that aligns with what matters to me. I feel nourished, and I feel empowered to make the decisions that make me feel rooted in my life.

Food helps communities root and grow, too. Imagine five women gathering in a warm kitchen for a food swap, sharing homemade food with each other. The table gets weighed down with peach and apple jams, bulbs of garlic, blueberry scones, sweet dumpling squash, canned corn, sauerkraut, venison sausage, three kinds of honey, maple syrup, dried beans and lentils, caramel sauce, and three types of bread. All homemade, homegrown, or harvested locally. At each monthly gathering of my neighborhood food swap, we take turns choosing one item at a time until everything has a new home. We've shared jams, jellies, marmalades, chutneys, relishes, pickles, pestos, spreads, sauces, beverages, wines, a huge variety of preserved fruits and vegetables, granolas, breads, eggs, goat soap, goat cheese, honey, and syrup. Seasonal fresh produce from the garden is a staple. A great soup someone made too much of is a welcome respite from one night of cooking for someone else who has a busy week. Beeswax candles or honey from some local hives are little reminders of what is possible when food is sourced with awareness.

The location changes monthly, and we have become friends. New members are welcomed wholeheartedly. We know each other's pantries, gardens, and kitchens. The goal of the food swap is to promote and share the energy that builds from making things and then sharing the results with each other. Good conversations are had, and ideas and knowledge are shared. Each month, we celebrate how good it feels to make our own food and share with others instead of buying whatever is on sale at the local big box store.

Alchemy is defined as *a seemingly magical process of transformation, creation, or combination.* There is a certain magic in sharing food, especially food that was mindfully grown and prepared. To cook and share is deeply human. When we share that process of transformation with others, we're part of the cycle of life.

### OTHER VOICES

Ramps, or wild onions, grow for two months in the Appalachian Mountains, where Carrie grew up. Today, seeing a ramp reminds her of her childhood. She enjoys connecting with the people behind her food by looking at the info tags in the grocery and getting to know the farmers at the farmers market. Being mindful of what and who's behind her food reminds her who she is and where she comes from.

Staying mindful of the essential gift of food roots us. For me, this means cooking and baking and growing a lot of my own vegetables. Sometimes I cook or bake every single day for weeks on end. When that happens, it's fantastic. Of course, some weeks it just doesn't happen like that. Yet, my presence in the process when it happens is more important than the *number of times* I cook something up from scratch. I try to engage in the act of making something from simple ingredients, paying attention to all aspects of the process. This allows me to see the good that comes from the work of my hands and a little patience. Of course, cooking and growing a garden isn't everyone's story, and that's okay. On the days or weeks when cooking just doesn't come into play, we still have to eat. There's always opportunity to do so with intention.

If it's available to us, we can choose to embrace the benefits of sourcing fruits, vegetables, and other food items from places closer to home. We can try to do the bulk of our shopping at farmer's markets and small, locally-owned stores to supplement what is harvested from our gardens. We can experiment with planting our own seeds. We can partner with others in the community to get more fresh produce in the local corner store. We can become members of one of the many CSAs (community supported agriculture) that serve communities all over the country.

It can be easy to get lost in middle class America's sea of infinite choice. With enough money, you can get anything you want anytime you want it. Yet so many people I've met, those who grow, mix, chop, and knead themselves, and eat seasonally, feel better and have a stronger connection to the earth. We can choose with intention what we eat, how we prepare it, and how it is shared. Conscientious cooking helps build a better food system for all.

For a myriad of reasons, many people struggle to put the time, energy, money, and planning into cooking and eating well. Not everyone enjoys (or has the resources for) dreaming up recipes and preparing food with love. Yet food is universal, necessary, and extraordinary in its ordinariness. Food is required for life and growth, so how can folks who struggle with food build a healthy relationship with it? It takes significant effort to build a working relationship with how to eat after years of challenge. Even if it doesn't come easily, anyone can build the capacity to understand food's profundity, its ability to bind and nurture, its essentialness. We can approach food with humility and surround ourselves with people who are already at peace with food. We can befriend a bread baker. Making peace with food is possible.

Through my work as a wellness coach, I've come into contact with many people who have a complicated relationship with nourishing themselves. Some athletes are required to eat more and gain weight. Other athletes are required to eat less and lose weight. Some folks overeat when they are bored, others when they are sad, still others when they are stressed or happy. Food is a reward and is often used to celebrate. Fast food is cheap and organic food is expensive. Food deserts are real, and many people are hungry.

Whether we are lovers of or intimidated by food, the invitation to alchemy is realistic. It is accessible and within each individual's control. Mindfully eating can be a first step toward healing. When we taste our food intentionally, we learn to savor, and to associate the food more with how it makes us feel than how it tastes. When we chew slowly, our bodies are smart enough to want the good stuff in the amounts that serve best. We can look beyond the calories to the laughter at the table. We can develop new preferences, even after years of the same patterns. We can stop labeling food as "good" or "bad" and simply see it as food. Food can function beyond necessity.

## OTHER VOICES

Natalie started paying closer attention to the labels on nut butters in the grocery store. Struck by the number of additives, she decided to grind her own peanut butter. It was easy, cheap, and tasty. Experimenting, she can customize her peanut butter to her tastes and save money at the same time.

Ellie has shared with me that she is one of those folks who has a complicated relationship with food. For her, every meal is an opportunity to re-engage and do food better. She says that when food is going well, she feels more connected to her body and the earth. There is a sense of belonging to herself. She can get creative about how food is grown and shared. Rituals around food, like inviting newly-engaged couples over to roll homemade sushi or baking twenty pies each year to share with her friends and family on Thanks-giving morning, help. She nurtures the love of food for her children, inviting them into the kitchen and garden.

Being head chef isn't necessary to be part of the alchemy. We can engage in the experience of food, see our role in the transformation, the sharing, the magic that hap-pens around meals. Some mothers use their bodies to feed and nourish babies, but don't go on to make bespoke tod-dler meals. Others might stay out of the kitchen entirely, but use their gifts to pick the music, light the candles, pair the wine, set the table, and feed the conversation. Inviting people over to share in the bounty, laughing and swapping stories at the table, helps create something from scratch that feeds us holistically.

The goal to break bread mindfully is deeply good. The process of tasting food and adding intention to every step of the food process adds health and spice to life while tending to the earth with gentle compassion. Mindfulness is a challenge, one that requires daily practice. Alchemy is an invitation.

Sourcing, making, sharing, and eating food can be mag-ical. It builds community. It deepens family. It celebrates culture. It changes our lives and the lives of others. We have an opportunity to be a partner in the food system, not just a consumer. Whether it's by baking bread, canning toma-toes, accepting a cucumber from a neighbor, advocating for a more robust produce section in a local supermarket, or simply tasting food fully, when we use the choice that we have to engage with our food with intention, that's when the magic happens.

## ～♦～ THE TINY THING ～♦～
### An invitation to alchemy

The making, eating, and sharing of food can be a magical tool for bringing profound change into our lives.

—DEMETRIA PROVATAS[1]

Choose one meal or snack to eat while fully engaged in the act. Prepare the food with intention and think about how this food came to be in front of you, right now. Who grew it? How did it get to you? Who cooked or baked or mixed it? With whom are you sharing the experience? Tune into the food on your plate and notice the way it looks and smells. How do you feel prior to the first bite? Explore the flavors that pop in your mouth, the various textures, how you feel as you eat it, and how it satisfies your hunger. Slow down. Eat one piece of food at a time and pause in between bites. Notice how full awareness impacts the act of eating. Break bread, mindfully. This is everyday alchemy in practice.

---

1. Demetria Provatas, "Chocolate Alchemy." *Taproot Magazine*, issue 21: WEAVE, 2016.

## Body Practice

Once a day, notice the position of your tongue in your mouth. Pull it away from the roof of your mouth or the back of your teeth and invite it to relax. Recognize if doing this also helps release tension in your face, jaw and throat as well. Allow your calm tongue to model surrender in the rest of your body and being.

## In Reflection

* What comes to mind when you think about food?
* From where do you get most of your food?
* What sort of dining experience really satisfies your hunger?
* How do you feel when you pay attention to your food?
* What makes you feel nourished? Satisfied?
* What happens when you taste things fully?
* What sort of change would you like to see food bring about in your life?
* What is another tiny thing that could work to cultivate alchemy in your life?

# Style

\stīl\

*noun*

a manner of doing something

a distinctive appearance, typically determined by the principles according to which something is designed

Curate a life that aligns your radiant inner and outer beauty.

## Ellie

Have you ever walked into someone's home and instantly felt calm and happy? Have you ever thought, "Wow, you look amazing," when walking by a person wearing something you'd never buy? Humans are drawn to beauty. People living in a way that celebrates style are practicing an alignment of the inner and outer self that others recognize and appreciate.

### OTHER VOICES

When Heidi (not Barr) meets with her interior design clients, she lays out five objects to see which they are drawn to. Design is all about stealing, repurposing, transforming, and owning it. Heidi believes beauty is an innate part of us. There is style in where she goes to eat, where she shops, how she parents, what she wears, and the home she cultivates. She filters her style by saying, "I like that, but it's not mine. I like it, but I don't want it."

We all have style; some of us just practice it more boldly than others. Style can be discarded by some as frivolous, expensive, superficial, extra, or intimidating. Yet developing style is a worthy pursuit that deepens our roots. Cultivating a style is simply about being awake and aware of self and surroundings. Knowing our style can help us be responsible consumers. Celebrating our style can offer joy and beauty to a world not fit for the mundane.

When outlining this book, Heidi was quick to assign the chapter on style to me. "I don't have style," she laughed. But she does. She prides herself on not investing a ton of money in stuff, and she is not high fashion, but she practices a style that shows alignment with her values. I told her I would take the lead on the style chapter but pushed her to embrace her style. She reflected a bit, then told me this story:

One warm summer evening, Heidi was strolling down a city boulevard with some friends deciding where to eat. She was wearing a stretchy brown skirt, a fitted green tank top, and sandals she'd gotten in Morocco 15 years earlier for about two US dollars. The air felt sweet against her bare skin.

"Gosh, Heidi, I love your style," said one of her friends.

"Come again?" Heidi asked, surprised. She glanced at her friend sideways, thinking, *What? I have no style whatsoever.*

"You just look classic and put together."

Heidi doesn't like shopping. She buys clothes only when what she has is falling apart, has been eaten by the dryer, or has gone missing. She feels like she knows little to nothing about fashion. She does not try to keep up with the times. Yet despite this, her friend noticed a look and liked it. The outfit was simple, fit well, and was comfortable. She felt good in her skin and felt confident in who she was. That outfit represented beauty and ease.

Writing professor Verlyn Klinkenborg told my class, "Don't try too hard to create a [writing] style. Don't force it. Your style is simply what you notice about the world." Graduate school writers tend to overdo it. For example, we like David Foster Wallace so much that we overuse footnotes.

Or we use flowery language in an attempt to impress, but it falls short. The reader senses that we are faking it, trying to be someone else. It leaves the writing strung out and vulnerable. By asking us to reign it in a bit, Klinkenborg helped us find our authenticity of voice instead of us forcing a voice that is not our own. If twenty writers went to the same party one night, and all decided to write a story about it, we'd all write something different. We'd notice different things and include different details. He advised, "Stop trying to write like other writers and settle into paying attention to what you notice about the world. This becomes your style."

Style, then, has something to do with noticing and being attuned to what is noticed. It requires letting go of what isn't and embracing what is. Practicing style—attuning, aligning, and embracing—can be applied to so many areas of our lives. Take hair, for example. When I notice the nature of my hair, I can become more attuned to what it wants to do. It can take on a style that is in line with who I am at the moment. My hair has a unique color and wave that I can work with. Some days I may wish my hair was brown or curly, but it's not. My true style emerges from embracing the hair I was born with. Have you ever caught yourself spending lots of time manipulating your hair to do something it just doesn't want to do? How does this feel when compared to getting a cut that accentuates your hair in its natural state? Not only can we save time, effort, and frustration, we can feel naturally beautiful. Others may notice at a superficial level and at a deeper, more profound level.

### OTHER VOICES

As a teen, Juliet copied trends that weren't reflective of who she was. She felt uncomfortable and disconnected. Today, more confident, she embodies both edgy and classic, tomboy and sexy, for a look that she calls feminine grunge. "I dress for people who misunderstand me," she says. "I want them to take a second look and see the real me." Everything from her tube of lipstick to her coffee mug reflects her aesthetic.

Stylish people seem to feel comfortable in their own skin, like they are always in their natural habitat. They are comfortable and confident, exuding beauty and ease. We can build an entire life around beauty and ease. This doesn't mean life becomes easy, but it does mean that life is underlaid by the alignment that exudes our truth.

A woman wearing an amazing outfit has put a little time and energy into noticing her own body shape, her coloring, and her aesthetic. Her clothes are an outward celebration of her inner self. She is expressing herself with fashion, and the self-awareness, attention to alignment, and confidence she is practicing are appealing. My friend Shelly follows a fashion blog for short people. She is under five feet tall and always looks amazing. Her wardrobe is simple and strategic. She feels tall every day. My friend Steph cuts out pictures she likes from magazines. In the morning, she copies the model with items she already owns, celebrating her fiery personality with her own style of colorful layers and patterns. Putting a little bit of time and intentionality into style upfront can actually simplify life. Meanwhile, there is joy that comes from a sense of alignment, when style is an authentic external expression of internal beauty.

## OTHER VOICES

Steve has always been fashionable. He was the first kid in his high school with parachute pants. He'd raid his mom's drama costume closet, scan thrift stores, and pay attention to musicians like David Bowie and Prince. "You can approach style like any other form of self-improvement," he says. "Put some time in, be open to learning and think of it as a hobby. It's worth it. If you look good, you feel good."

At its best, style can also heal. My friend Nancy looked in the mirror and loathed what she saw. She didn't recognize herself. She felt out of touch with the woman she was before having babies. At that moment, her little daughter walked in the bedroom, gave her a hug and said, "You are my mommy girl!" A light went off for Nancy. She was a mommy, yes, but she was a girl, partner, sibling, marketing professional, and writer, too. She was more than one thing, and she could hold the person she was, is, and will be in her being. She did some self-care from the outside in. Putting on active clothes or professional clothes, for example, reminded her to cultivate not just her mommy-ness, but also the other aspects of her person. It was a tiny step toward building a style that celebrated her truest, layered self. We may find ourselves in a moment where we have to care for the self from the outside in and making choices about our outward life can help.

My own style journey hinges on noticing my unfolding sense of self through changing stages of life. Going to Catholic schools meant college was the first time I could experiment with a wardrobe. Even then, being a two-sport athlete, I spent half the day in sweaty, comfortable clothes. As a young girl, I dabbled in jewelry, spicing up my school uniform to express my personality and individuality. Then, as a young adult, at my first clothes swap, style's relation to alignment deepened for me.

I love getting a bunch of people together of different ages, professions, and styles. They bring clothes they don't wear much and encourage swapping. An expecting mom might get clothes from a woman who is newly done breast-feeding. A woman who wants to start running can get gear from someone pivoting to low impact yoga. What is a seven on one person may be a ten on the next person. Seeing an item that didn't work for me look stunning on someone with different proportions, coloring, or attitude taught me a lot about my own being. My style started to emerge.

**OTHER VOICES**

Kate was diagnosed with cancer at age three. Living without hair and wanting to feel feminine, she wore headbands and dresses while going through chemotherapy. Moving to New York embolden Kate's adult sense of style. "Clothing tells a story on your body, but also carries stories with it." Kate loves buying clothes at family estate sales, which enhances her sense of carrying other people's stories with her. Her style advice? Find a uniform that works with your body and own it.

Not only did my wardrobe get smaller, it got more strategic. More often I walked out of the house feeling confident. My clothes became an extension of myself, a celebration of my specific body and being. I wasn't trying to be someone else; I was more deeply expressing me. My fiery friend, Steph, told me my element was fire, too. She's right. When I wear fall colors and use loud patterns and colors, people recognize the alignment between my spirit and my clothes. I feel awake, like my inside is being expressed, like I am adding beauty to the world. As a teacher, I started Fun Pants Fridays where I'd wear crazy pants to end the week. On big days, I wear big outfits. I want to show my students you can be smart and stylish, and that you can look good with an intentional wardrobe built from thrift stores. Staying awake to who I am and honoring my body with my style invites those around me to do the same.

So, wear the red socks, the pearls, or the flats instead of heels. Or the heels instead of flats. Wear at least one thing that says, "Yep. This is me. This is what makes me feel good. This is me choosing to align with my inner beauty."

Style does not need to start or end with clothes. Building an aesthetic in our home and life can add calm and pleasure as we move through our days in alignment. Take my green couch, for example. When my spouse's grandmother died, we inherited her seventy-year-old green couch. It is a loud green, true vintage in a way that IKEA is trying to replicate. It's heavy and high quality. We'll have it until we die. We took a long look at the couch and the room it was in, and in tune with our aesthetic, slowly started building a room that had a mid-century style from other items we owned. People always comment on that room as being calming and pleasant in its minimalism and clean lines. We took notice of the space and the couch and built a stylish room that brings joy.

We can fill our spaces in a style that brings us joy. The trick is to celebrate the self without getting lost in stuff. Can we live without the stuff? Is it still non-essential to our sense of worth? Makeup, for example, is part of my style. Some days call for playful eyeshadow, others for just a natural lip gloss. I use it to accentuate what is already there, not to change it, so I look more like me, not less. I monitor how much money I spend on makeup, and how much time I spend applying it. There are plenty of days I don't wear makeup, and I don't feel like I need it to look beautiful or to feel like me. The stuff can't become a superficial veneer to hide behind, but should point to the truth.

The amount of stuff we have matters. In the world of fast fashion, there is a new look out every week, adding more textile items to landfills than ever. An overflowing closet or a cluttered room can distract from beauty. Style can be a meaningful filter that keeps our purchasing informed and in line with our values. To harness our own sense of style—the one that keeps us focused on what matters, from wardrobe to home decor—we may need to get rid of what doesn't work first and then get enough of what does. Asking what is enough is always a valid question. We can move toward comfort and confidence while also recognizing factory conditions and the reality of a finite planet.

The quality of the stuff we have also matters. In the documentary *The Minimalists*, sociologist Juliet Schor says, "We are too materialistic in the everyday sense of the word, and we are not at all materialistic enough in the true sense of the word. We need to be true materialists, like really care about the *materiality* of goods." Style begs us to think about the quality of our material goods. Do we need it? Do we use it?

Will it last? Is it true to our aesthetic? Does it bring us joy? As authors, podcasters, and filmmakers Joshua Fields Millburn and Ryan Nicodemus, also knowns as *The Minimalists* point out, "Love people and use things. The opposite never works." If we love the stuff and not the self, the self will fade.

The alignment in style is about valuing beauty enough to build a beautiful life. Deeper, more vibrant, more essential than prettiness, beauty is long-lasting and nourishing. Style is about reflecting the pride we have in the beautiful life we are curating. It's about surrounding ourselves with life-giving people, places, and things and then allowing that light to shine from the inside out. It is an expression of our unique being and spirit. It is a gift to ourselves and to others.

## THE TINY THING
### An invitation to alignment

Fashion changes, but style endures.[1]

–Coco Chanel

Pick an area of your life where there is external expression and stuff—your wardrobe, your shoe collection, your home décor, or your book collection, for example.

---

1. Coco Chanel, quoted in Dominique Loreau, *L'art de la Simplicité: How to Live More with Less* (New York: St. Martin's Press, 2017).

Choose one item in that category that is not in alignment with your inner self. Notice what about that thing is out of line. Do you remember why you got it? Find a new, more strategic home for the object. Then find one item that does bring you joy, that does express you. Notice a sense of style emerging and celebrate that extension of yourself.

## Body Practice

Once a day, consciously tilt your chin up and pull your chin back just a bit more than usual. Then gently reach the crown of your head toward the sky. Live out of the power and ease of alignment.

## In Reflection

* Who is the most stylish person you know? How is that style expressed?
* What is one item of clothes that you feel amazing in? Why?
* What is one room of your house that you love spending time in? Why?
* What is an item of clothing that you purchased with someone else's style in mind? How does it make you

feel when you wear it? Is it empowering, or does it make you feel self-conscious?

* What is one area of your life that feels in alignment, a true extension of yourself?

* What is one area of your life where you'd like to develop a sense of style? What is a good first step?

* How can you become more materialistic in the sense of the word—really thinking about the quality of the material your things are made out of?

* What is another tiny thing that could work to cultivate alignment in your life?

*Six*

# Nature

\\'nāCHər\\

*noun*

the phenomena of the physical world collectively, including plants, animals, the landscape, and other features and products of the earth

Look to wildness. There is healing there.

## Heidi

Late summer, in a year with enough rain, life outside in the American Midwest is thriving. Every branch is reaching its leaves toward the sky, and every root is nestling deep into the soil, drinking up the ample nourishment that comes with abundant moisture and compost. The sunflowers in my garden tower over me, flower heads following the sun as it arcs across the sky. They end the day gazing toward the westerly hills. There are basketball-sized cabbages, canopies of kale shading the voles who munch the beets, and if all of the winter squash and zucchini vines were stretched out in a line, they would reach down the road and around the corner. Bees and hummingbirds buzz about, happily drinking up raspberry and oregano blossom nectar, doing their important pollinating work. Peppers, tomatoes, and eggplants offer their fruits, and the potato plants start to lean over in hopes of harvest. The beavers are doing their work, too, as the keepers of the lake, and lily pads have fully claimed the shallows. Herons stalk fish, and flocks of wild turkeys saunter the fields. Children dart between garden rows with bare feet and hide behind bouquets of prairie grass and clover. Even ditch wildflowers declare themselves worthy of noticing.

Life outside is thriving. When I can remember how much life, abundance, beauty, and wonder exists just outside the door, I thrive, too.

I don't always remember.

The melancholy of modernity can be pretty persistent.

In fact, if you could read my mind, there would be days you'd think I was destitute, completely alone, walking across the Sahara with no water. Or on an iceberg near

Greenland, with no boats in sight, a severe dislike of fish, and a low tolerance for cold temperatures. It's so easy to forget abundance—to forget that I, too, am a creature. I forget that I come from wildness, that we humans originated as part of nature, rather than just being visitors on the weekends, from four to six on Tuesday evenings, or during an annual camping trip.

### OTHER VOICES

Alissa intentionally observes and connects with wild-life. She imagines what it's like to live like a bird in the branches or like a whale in the ocean. She watches her non-human neighbors move and experience life to gain new perspectives on how she can live. Animals remind her to root into her senses to see the world in a different way.

This is where remembering comes into play. Remembering that my roots are interwoven with wildness helps me slough off the bleak moods. Just as trees reach toward the sky and root into the soil, when I step into nature, my body involuntarily does the same. I inhale, and the crown of my head reaches ever so slightly more toward the sky. I exhale, and energy flows through my feet into the earth. We all have a bit of wildness in us that recognizes the wildness in the natural world. The wildness in me recognizes the wildness in you. Nature recognizes all of us as fellow creatures, gently healing us, reminding us of our smallness carved in relief of the vastness of creation. Wildness invites us back into the interconnectedness of our ecosystem. We are a part of something bigger, cleverer, and more beautiful than any single organism. The breeze hushes, the earth cradles, the sun calls.

As modern humans, we tend to spend a great deal of time removed from the earth, from the rhythms of the natural world. It's all too easy to forget that at the end of the day, we are part of this great web of life. We can invent amazing things—technology has taken us perhaps further than we thought we'd ever be able to go. But I often wonder what we lose when we forget where we came from. What do we miss when we stop noticing the ants and bees and crows and lichen? What do we miss when we refuse to let the rain fall on our skin, when we stop walking barefoot in the mud, when we don't let our children run freely in the woods? Wildness, as much as modern culture wants us to believe otherwise, is an integral part of what makes us human. A deep part of our being suffers when we lose sight of that. Dirt calms us (and gives us essential microbes). Sun awakens us (and gives us vitamin D). Beauty softens us. Nature invites us to dwell. To root. To rise. Feeling connected to the natural world simply makes us feel better.

Something that makes me feel connected to the natural world, if I had to choose just one thing, is a sense of wonder. That feeling of awe that makes me realize that I am, in a single breath, vast and tiny, mortal and immortal, one of many living beings on a living planet. From a foundation of wonder, we go about our days with a sense of abundance and compassion for others. We're more resilient. Calmer. Healthier. Wonder is a survival skill, one that helps us thrive.

## OTHER VOICES

Jessy takes her dogs out every morning on the trails behind her house. They patrol and hunt while she soaks up the quiet and the smell of the pines. Regular time outside gets her out of the modern blur. She pays attention to her body and takes time to face the grace and challenge the natural world provides, keeping her grounded in reality.

In a world that makes it easy to keep our heads down, focused just on what we can see through the human-made lens (devices, schedules, what people have created), nature invites us to look up. All the way up. It's good for the soul to spend some time looking toward the heavens in wonder. What if we took more time to look up at the stars? Could we feel aligned with other curious humans over thousands of years who looked *all the way up* to wonder about the moon and the galaxies? Claiming a place in wildness invites that sense of connectedness. It invites us to reach in all directions and come back to ground-level with renewed, refreshed perspective.

Cultivating wonder is as easy as stepping outside, and children are excellent teachers when it comes to doing this. Every single day, no matter what the weather forecaster says, I make a point to head outside, often with my young daughter leading the way. So does Ellie, with her sons. Children are in touch with their creatureliness. They look up at the cloudless sky and down at the burrowing worms with a sense of wonder. They gleefully embrace whatever nature offers. They find gifts in the wild web of life.

Human beings of all ages need to interact with that web of life. We need to embrace our own wildness, to put on snow or mud boots, wiggle toes in the soil, gaze at the stars, or sit on the front step to look at the clouds. We're a small part of this tapestry of matter that makes up the planet we call home. It is worth it to practice leaning into that sense of wonder, to practice paying attention to what's going on in the great outdoors. Some days this is easy, and some days this is hard. Some days it doesn't happen. I've noticed there's a marked difference in how I feel on the days that I allow a busy schedule or the weather to keep me indoors.

If I'm in a bad mood, my spouse typically says, "Have you been outside yet today?" He knows that doing so will make me feel better. When I am in a haze of wanting something different, or feel dissatisfied or filled with dread, going outside helps. Some folks I know actually put a reminder in their calendar to pop up in the middle of the afternoon that simply says, "Go outside." A walk through the woods probably won't change what's wrong, but it *can* change how we respond to it. It opens a door to feeling what needs to be felt while also offering solace via fresh air.

Think about it for a moment: What changes in your interaction with life when you set aside a frustrating task to turn fresh strawberries over in your hand on a hot day, lifting them to your face to inhale the sweetness of their bodies into yours? Or when you let rushing water caress your bare ankles as you wade in a creek after a tough day at work? Or when you close your eyes and listen to what trees or wind or birds have to say, especially when relationships with other people feel strained? Fresh air, movement, and connection with nature have been proven by numerous studies to improve mood, even if we opt to go outside begrudgingly. Something I say to my coaching clients all the time is, "trust that you do not need motivation to do something—you just have to do it." Nature is a willing companion, always reminding, inviting, and healing us into well-being. Nature doesn't care if you are in a bad mood as long as you show up, willing to allow wildness to do its work in you.

In South Korea, scientists are working to resurrect and clone the prehistoric woolly mammoth from preserved specimens found in Siberia. Scientists Sergey Zimov and Nikita Zimov believe that introducing the woolly mammoth to graze the tundra can help slow down the rapidly melting permafrost there. Melting permafrost releases methane and carbon dioxide into the atmosphere, having huge implications for (even more) accelerated climate change. The animals currently grazing the tundra, like elk, bison, and yaks, thin the snow and make it denser, which helps it freeze deeper. The sheer size and weight of the woolly mammoth would simply be more effective.

### OTHER VOICES

Drew suffers from seasonal depression. One of their tools to combat the downward spiral is to go winter camping. "Being outside helps me embrace the darkness and take full advantage of the light," Drew says. The fresh air and the act of dealing with the elements wake their being up and gets an inner fire going, helping them stay present to the cold, dark winter of Minnesota.

Pleistocene Park, a nature reserve in Siberia founded by Sergey Zimov, is an experiment in reestablishing ecosystems. It hinges on the belief that creatures and the earth can work together toward health if given the freedom and space away from humans to do so. There are, of course, many unknowns and mixed opinions on the ethics and viability when it comes to using human technology like cloning to manipulate nature, even if intentions are noble. No one knows what the long-term outcomes of an experiment like Pleistocene Park will be, but we do know that nature, from creatures and plants and microbes and ancient rock, has an inherently healing quality to it.

When we attune to the earth as creatures, live in harmony with wildness, and appreciate nature, we can work toward healing. Take, for example, Kathy and Dave whose daughter died tragically when she had her whole life ahead of her. To cope and grieve, they travel to places like Glacier National Park together to dwell in nature. It helps them feel small, which somehow offers the slightest bit of comfort. Walking on the green earth reminds them that they, too, are creatures that can find healing in the earth. When Rachel miscarried, she spoke of an undeniable desire to go outside and bleed into the dirt, to offer the life force and potential back to the earth. Kirsten takes a morning run on the beach in bare feet. The sand between her toes sustains her. The vastness of the ocean soothes her. With the water lapping at her feet, she never feels alone. Babies often calm when taken outside. We, too, can stop spiraling, feeling stuck, or feeling claustrophobic if we turn to nature for a sense of peace. We remember what it feels like to come back to ourselves. We root.

One late autumn day, I took the canoe out on the tiny lake behind my house. Brilliant light bounced off of gold foliage. I could see my breath as the air cooled. The sun dipped behind the trees as I paddled slowly through the shallow, lily-pad-studded water. An enormous snapping turtle, her shell covered in bumps and moss, swam directly under the canoe (I was glad to be in a boat.). Her presence reminded me of all the life that exists outside my window, outside my screens, outside my human-focused agenda, outside my anxiety and worry and bad moods. I saw part of myself in her wildness, and she made me want to be a better human, a better planetary neighbor, a better ancestor.

Our existence is dwelling in the tension between reaching and rooting, the ever-present and sacred dance. Walking on the earth, and feeling totally alive, brings with it humility, perspective, and softness necessary for compassion. Nature lures us to a higher self. Reaching and rooting with the trees, we dwell in the present moment and find, often through wonder, a true sense of enough.

### OTHER VOICES

Ben's spirituality is deeply tied to nature, and he passes on his love of wildness to his children. He'll rope off a one-foot by one-foot square of his backyard and study it aloud with his son, naming everything that is happening in the tiny patch of land. Likewise, with his daughter, because she is curious to know how everything works, Ben takes apart plants and talks her through the organisms. He uses nature to remind his children and himself that they are all creatures that are inherently good and deserve compassion.

Think about moments of being hushed by the age-less wisdom of the mountains, or marveling at the renew-ing power of smelling pine while sweating out toxins on a walk through the woods or laughing with inexplicable joy as water from a waterfall soaks your face. Minds quiet the moment the canoe paddle hits the water. Shoulders relax and eyes adjust to the welcoming sunshine of the backyard.

Wonder can be part of our routine, a routine that affords a chance to see tiny orange mushrooms atop fallen oaks, enormous trees that crashed to earth years ago, in death covered with soft moss and craggy lichen, a demon-stration of resurrection.

It can mean eating blackberries, those whose bram-bles tower high overhead, hanging heavy with fruit, tiny orbs tasting of sunlight and wild nectar and delight. It can mean following the tracks of rabbits, deer, and squirrels through the snow as it crunches under our boots. It can mean hearing a breeze rustling leaves high in the maples, a chorus of gentle giants celebrating what life is like in the canopy. It can mean feeling the feet of a caterpillar tickling bare skin as the fuzzy being makes a path on new territory. It can mean smelling earthy loam underfoot, the sharp-ness of hot pine, the richness of last year's leaves mixed with the forest floor's moisture, hints of rain in the air, a reminder of how refreshment can sneak up on a person. It can mean allowing tears to well up from somewhere unknown, streaming down, dropping to earth, wildness and humanness melting together.

Feel the sunshine on your skin. Notice the color of the leaves. Wander. Listen. Take an intentional breath of outdoor air. Touch something wild. When I do those things, it's enough to snap me out of melancholy. It reminds me of all the things that are worth celebrating during the days that I spend here on this earth.

Late autumn cold, though not unexpected, is often startling in the Midwest. Despite the chill, it feels good to walk through fields that have provided nourishment of all sorts to beings of all kinds. Ice clings to stalks of bowing grass. Every step crunches in the stillness of the freeze. Muted colors announce themselves in burnt umber, dark brown, and burgundy, reminding us that decline holds its own subtle, often uncelebrated, beauty. Sunflowers that have grown to maturity tower overhead, brittle seed-heads declaring themselves done for now. Signs of humans intersecting with earth pepper the landscape, steel and wire and old tarps, reminding us that we are not just walking in nature. We are what nature is doing, which comes with a responsibility to walk in ways that honor ourselves and every other living thing. A cold wind rustles dry corn stalks. Two hawks fly toward the river. It is a time to savor what it's like to be present to a place, to be attuned to how wildness can work in a human life. In late autumn, booted (rather than bare) feet kiss the

ground, and if we walk lightly, they leave footprints of wonder in our wake.

Every day we can choose between scarcity and abundance, between a stupor and being awake, between crabby
and wonder. The sound of the wind, the feel of the sun,
and the sight of plants can punctuate even the dreariest
days with one more detail that makes life worth celebrating.
Notice the beauty that pierces the ordinary days. Go outside. Even in the middle of the biggest city on the planet, all
we have to do is look up to the sky to reclaim the wildness
that is still there, even amidst the concrete. It is inviting us
to remember our roots.

Step outside. Come into contact with something wild.
There is healing there.

### ᴿᵉᵉᵉ THE TINY THING ᴿᵉᵉᵉ
#### An invitation to wildness

We need the tonic of wildness.[1]

–Henry David Thoreau

Open the door and step outside. Stand directly on the
earth, if the weather conditions allow, and feel the ground

---

1. Henry David Thoreau, *Walden* (Boston: Ticknor and Fields, 1854).

with your feet. If that's not an option, touch a nearby tree with your fingertips or pick up a rock. Come into contact with something wild, something that is not human made. Welcome the fresh air and just stand or sit there for a few moments. Notice how you feel without judgment and notice what's going on with whatever bit of nature is at your fingertips or under your toes. If the only natural material you have available is the sky, then look up. Drink in the sky with your eyes or feel the outdoor air on your skin.

To feel truly rooted in our lives as human beings, we have to make a point to remember that we are a part of nature, not just creatures using the earth to keep our bodies alive. To remember this and get the idea to stick to your bones, it helps to go outside and marvel at the wonders of the natural world, no matter where you are.

Step outside and feel outdoor air on skin for five minutes. Marvel. Feel it fully, whether it's uncomfortable, delicious, scorching, or frigid. Try not to judge what you are feeling and just let it exist, welcome it, and invite it to be part of the day. Repeat as needed until wonder becomes part of the routine. We can be a sense of wonder embodied.

## Body Practice

Once a day, hum. Close your eyes, place your hands on your throat and chest, and send your vibration out into the world. On your inhales, sense the abundance of your environment. Receive the beauty and generosity of the universe around you and allow it to bring you energy, healing, and peace. Then hum for one more exhale, sending gratitude and you-ness back in response.

## In Reflection

* How do you feel when you spend time outside?
* What does nature do for you?
* What would happen if you spent more time outside embracing things that seem a little "wild"?
* What makes you feel connected to the earth?
* Where do you find wonder?
* What turns your mood around when you are feeling bleak?
* What helps you "survive" the trials of modern life?
* What is another tiny thing that could work to cultivate wildness in your life?

# Seven

# Communication

\kəˌmyo͞onəˈkāSH(ə)n\
*noun*

the imparting or exchanging of information or news

Healthy communication fosters seeing and
being seen.

## Ellie

"Which of your five senses is the most underutilized?" I asked a group of teenagers at a retreat. It was meant to be a warm-up question to get at the amazing things our bodies can do, but it immediately spawned a poignant conversation.

"My sight," one young woman replied immediately. "I don't look at things."

"Tell me more," I said.

"Seriously, my face is always buried in my phone. I forget to see."

She made an astute distinction between looking at her phone and truly seeing. As she scrolls through her feeds, her seeing is often passive consumption. Using similar logic, the next student said her phone distracts her from listening. Passive hearing versus active listening. Over and over, students articulated that a tool meant for communication was limiting it.

Technology is not inherently limiting to communication. It has the potential to build relationships and connections in ways we never before dared to dream. A young woman who is experimenting with identifying as queer finds a life-giving online community where she feels safe. A young man finds a writing group online who appreciates science fiction, and the members become his second family. At the same time, year after year, teenagers get singled out and bullied brutally online. School culture has followed kids home, making it inescapable. The teenagers at the retreat explained the unwritten rules of living online, like having more followers than people you follow. A self-assured junior admits that she ties the amount of likes an image gets to her self-worth. She is constantly comparing her stats to others, and she can't figure out what she's doing wrong. People working with teenagers think about how to approach technology with a healthy caution. Our media-saturated lives offer us daily reasons to respect the power of technology as a communication tool that we can use, for better and for worse. If we are intentional in our use of it, we can set boundaries so that technology enhances and deepens our lives instead of distracting us from the good stuff.

### OTHER VOICES

When his phone broke, Noah decided not to buy a new one. He deactivated his Facebook account for a year after realizing the deep hold it had on his concept of self as it relates to others. After the 2016 election, the polarized comments reached a toxic level on his feed. During Lent, he committed to having one conversation a week face to face with someone who thought differently about a political or religious issue.

Every time I ask young people to put their phones away for an hour discussion, a weekend retreat, or even a ten-day educational trip, they love the freedom they feel. They love what they see and the conversations that become possible. Communicating without technology requires vulnerability, which is an essential component of real community. Once we return to life as usual, it's hard to carve out that freedom for ourselves. It requires proactive boundary-setting, which will look different for everyone. All it takes is thinking about etiquette and boundaries—treating each other well and being able to unplug.

This is not a teenage conversation. We stop a fun moment with a friend to document it, post it, and circle back to check on its likes. Our kids ask us to play with them instead of taking pictures of them playing. We answer texts and emails during work meetings, meals, and even while sitting on the toilet. Kids tug at the clothes of parents looking into their phones, call to them with increasing volume, wanting their eye contact and attention. We easily get distracted at work and at home, with free time we admit is not always life-giving.

Adults are just grown kids and adjusted teenagers. We crave intimacy and connection, yet often feel isolated and alone. We struggle to authentically communicate and long to be seen and listened to. Technology can help in ways we never imagined a few generations ago. It can also hold us back. We, too, are trying to navigate what role technology should be playing in our lives.

When I lived far away from home, I Skyped with my nephews across the country. I played catch, pretending to throw a ball back and forth across the abyss. I played hide and seek, my spouse hiding while I carried the laptop where the little ones told me to. A friend of mine opened email accounts for his two children that they will get access to when they turn eighteen. He writes to them on special occasions like their birthdays. When my first child was born and I was home on leave, I felt far away from my spouse. My days were filled with feeding, cuddling, cooing and diaper changing. His days were filled with meetings, computers, adult conversation, dress clothes, and project management. The distance between our realities was vast, and it felt unbalanced. When my spouse left work, he texted me and let me know he was on his way home. We both spent his commute time imagining how the other's day may have gone. I pictured the good and the bad of an office workday. He imagined the joy and the struggle of a day with a newborn. By the time he walked through the door, we greeted each other with warmth, curiosity, and openness. We asked each other about how the day went and were ready to really hear the answer. We grew in empathy and compassion. We were patient with each other and more in tune with what the other needed in the evening to get up and do it all over again the next day. It helped us see each other.

Yet like teens, I curate my feeds, posting happy, becoming photos of vacations and accomplishments online. Every time I stop to take a picture, I leave the moment to document the moment. I share an article and think my justice work is complete. I take shortcuts instead of investing in the hard work of communication. I send old friends prepared stock messages like "Congrats on the work anniversary" with a simple click, while I long for a deeper connection.

More than depth of communication is at stake. This is a matter of seeing. Seeing and being seen brings the humanity and dignity we crave. If left unchecked, our online lives can lead us to objectification and fragmentation of the self. There is a distance between the self and the projected self. Does our online profile tell the true story of our lives? Is how we are seen more important than who we are? There is discrepancy between the two-dimensional story and reality. Honoring the difference between virtual reality and reality can encourage an authentic and accurate sense of self so we do not equate the flat profile with the sacred being. Zadie Smith warns, "When a human being becomes a set of data on a website like Facebook, he or she is reduced. Everything shrinks. We lose our bodies, our messy feelings, our desires, our fears . . . our denuded networked selves don't look more free, they just look more owned."[1]

Sometimes the ones we love the most are the hardest to really see. Sometimes they are the easiest ones with whom to take shortcuts. Technology has the ability to enhance and deepen intimacy that is already established. It can help us build compassion and aid in us seeing the other. It works best when we are willing to back it up with the hard work of sacred communication. My friend, Michelle, grew apart from her father and couldn't seem to find common ground. Hurtful

---

1. Zadie Smith, "Generation Why?" *The New York Review of Books*, (November 25, 2010).

things were said. They stopped discussing religion and politics, which eventually limited even more topics. Small talk left her wanting for more intimacy and real communication. Instead of shutting down, she got curious about his story. She asked to take his oral history, and over the course of her interviews, she grew in compassion and understanding for her father. He had a remarkable story filled with hurt and struggle. She started to see him more clearly. They are slowly working toward more compassionate communication.

**OTHER VOICES**

Ester spent a year completely off of the internet. She decided something had to shift in her personal and professional life. In resetting her life, she had to communicate with her family, friends, and community in completely new ways. She wrote letters, struck up conversations with strangers, and even got to know God. By interacting with the world without any help from internet-driven technology, she regained clarity and found peace.

Shortly after her grandmother moved to memory care, Heidi found a wooden jewelry box in her parents' garage. There was a handwritten note with her grandma's name on it tucked alongside dangly earrings, gemstone bracelets, and broaches. The note was from Heidi's grandfather who had been dead for twenty years. The paper was yellowed. The words were written in cursive with an ink pen. It read, "To my dearest wife: Occasionally through history a man is privileged to have a wife who is special above most other people—kind, understanding, gentle, with a quality born of an inner sense of goodness. I know this isn't a great big gift—money couldn't buy a gift big enough to express my feelings for you. Thanks for being who you are. I love you." Sitting in an overstocked garage with the note in hand, Heidi felt transported through time. The physicality and handwriting were intimate. He saw her, and we can only imagine that she felt seen.

Heidi thought of that piece of paper when her then-boyfriend, Nick, started a journal for the two of them. He wrote his reflections about meeting Heidi and the goings on at the camp where they worked that summer. He gave it to her on Valentine's Day. They passed it back and forth, each keeping it for a few months at a time. They filled the pages with the ordinary, everyday stuff like how they were feeling at work, what the weather was like, or how hard it was to live with roommates. They wrote about the extraordinary, like the evolutions of their feelings, their insecurities about where life might lead, their love for this other human. They felt the mutual joy of loving someone who loves you back. They saw each other and wanted to stay.

Years later, in a tiny lake-side cottage, Nick handed Heidi the little red notebook. She took it from him and flipped open to the last page to be greeted with the words, "Will you marry me?" He was down on one knee. They still have the journal, an artifact of their courtship and a reminder to continue to communicate intentionally with one another.

How can handwritten letters inform our communication? What if we wrote a letter to our moms or siblings instead of just posting a quick picture on Instagram or Facebook? What if we wrote a love note on real paper, even after ten years of marriage? We want to see and be seen. We want to really listen and feel heard. How we interact with others has the power to invite a bit of the sacred into each exchange when that exchange is punctuated by intention and compassion. True communication transforms us. That can happen on paper or via a screen.

Part of our work as digital citizens is addressing compassionate communication in the two-dimensional world. We can ask three important questions to help us foster a healthy relationship with our devices and that also nourishes seeing and compassionate communicating. All three questions are asking us to stay awake to our senses:

*Who is behind the screen?* It helps to remember that online interactions are human interactions, and there is a feeling person on the other side of the screen. Can you see the other?

*What story are you telling?* What parts of your life are appropriate for public consumption? We heavily curate our stories, and the two-dimensional version of you is not the real you. Only seeing the happiest, most becoming ten percent of people's lives in our feeds can make us feel even more isolated and depressed. Unchecked with a self-awareness, we can reflect on our own lives with eyes of scarcity that leave us wanting. Can you see yourself?

*Can you unplug?* It is not about just limiting screen time because not all screen time is equal. Research does show, however, that people who can totally unplug from time to time tend to do better in life. Can you see the world around you?

Teenagers are at a very important stage of development where they are cleaving from their families and building intimacy with their peers. Major identity formation is happening as their bodies and minds stretch and change. When I lead discussions with teenagers around healthy relationships, we talk at length about the different types of intimacy—mental, emotional, spiritual, physical, and sexual—and how we can build healthy intimate relationships with our peers. To model this, I do an activity called speed dating. I have youth sit in two circles—the inner facing the outer—and they have a series of one on one conversations. I provide the topic, but I also give the youth ample time to move on to other topics before the circles rotate to find a new conversation partner. They think about their own body language while listening and ask questions of the other person that comes from a place of curiosity. It is a practiced skill to be able to ask a question that the other person wants to answer. It requires real listening to build a conversation and real seeing to recognize when the other person is lighting up. The art of conversation can be practiced. Every time speed dating is coming to a close, the teenagers tell me how fun it is and ask when they can do it again. "You can do it anytime you want," I reply, "you are just talking to each other."

We know it's not that easy. They like being required to talk to people they aren't supposed to talk to. They like that time is set aside and they are given a few relational tools to try. They get that they are being taught how to see each other, and everyone likes to feel seen.

I count myself as a student of seeing clearly. My children are two of my teachers. Raising young children is exhausting in part because they are listening so intently to everything that I say and don't say. I have to work harder to listen to my baby who can't talk, yet communicates so purely and clearly, often more effectively than adults who have words. They appreciate when I see them. My young son studies the still pictures in books so intently and at such depth of detail with pure curiosity. He tells me when he's ready for me to turn the book page, and after we read a book, he will go back to the beginning and want to just look at it, asking questions about what's happening in the pictures beyond what the words say. When we are on walks out in the world, he looks slowly. He sees entire stories that I miss. I love honoring and nurturing his peripheral vision. He is teaching me how to see.

As a writer, in a way I am a professional communicator. My role as a sibling, friend, partner, and parent requires healthy communication, too. It helps to really look at the volume and quality of time I spend on social media. I don't want to prove that I'm living my life. I want to be more present to the life I am living. I don't want to fragment myself between how I'm really doing and how the online community may passively intuit I'm doing. It helps to remind myself of what function each technological tool serves, making sure it adds value to work and life. Inevitably, I need the reminder to unplug, slow down and show up to my three-dimensional life.

### OTHER VOICES

After Susan and Jon had children, they felt a distance in their marriage that stemmed from less intentional communication. They committed to a new daily practice of waking up before their kids, brewing coffee, and having quiet time together. At times, this meant rising as early as 4:00am, but it became a ritual they looked forward to and leaned on. The investment has paid off. The careful daily communication also inspired them to get nonviolent communication training as a whole family.

Rob, a coworker of mine, asks students to handwrite papers because it slows them down enough to leave more room for thinking. Mike, another coworker, will go find us instead of sending an email when the content is sensitive to make sure we are hearing his tone and seeing his body language. It seems inefficient in the short term, but it fosters healthy communication in the long term. There's a time to move fast and a time to slow down. A time to reach out across the abyss and a time to love the one you are with. A time to stay on the surface, texting a sibling about logistics, and a time to dwell in the depth of another, laughing and crying in the presence of a beloved. If we are spending too much time in the world of fast surface consumption in person or online, our communication muscles can atrophy, and our relationships can become more superficial and less vulnerable as well. Striving to communicate with integrity, committing to seeing and being seen, is a slow art that requires vulnerability, brings dignity, and fosters healthy community.

## ～～ THE TINY THING ～～
### An invitation to see

Being listened to is so closely connected to being loved that most of us feel they are one in the same.
—DAVID W. AUGSBURGER[2]

Hand write a letter to someone you care about. Take your time. Ask questions you think the person will be excited

2. David W. Augsburger, *Caring Enough to Be Heard* (Raleigh: Regal Books, 1982).

to answer. Share details about different facets of your life not everyone gets to see. Writing letters shows intentionality, forethought, and generosity. It creates an artifact with the sacredness of your handwriting and the feel of real paper. It takes time. It embraces well-articulated sentiment and carefully chosen words. Real communication takes practice, and a letter allows the reader to ingest it at their own pace. To get a better friend, be a better friend.

## Body Practice

Once a day, when you sense your mind being pulled in multiple directions, close your eyes for a few moments. Let your eyeballs drop back in their sockets. Find your body, your center again. Then open your eyes slowly. With eyes refreshed and mind quiet, grounded in the moment, see anew.

## In Reflection

* Who in your life makes you feel seen and heard? How?
* Who have you stopped seeing clearly?
* What helps you see clearly and fully?
* Who do you struggle to communicate with?

* How do you use technology to enhance and deepen intimacy that is already established?
* How are you leaning too hard on technology and forgetting to do the hard work of sacred communication?
* What happens when you slow the pace of your correspondence? How about when you speed it up?
* What is another tiny thing that could work to cultivate communication in your life?

# Home

\hōm\
*noun*

the place where one lives permanently

Gratitude, embodied, is to find home within.

## Heidi

The house I grew up in is a wood-sided, passive solar structure that my father built himself. Perched on the side of a prairie hillside, two wood stoves were the main heat sources. We had a composting toilet until I was in elementary school when Dad put in a septic system by hand. Days in the summer were spent outside in the fields around the five-acre plot, picking berries and vegetables in the garden and strategically placing Breyer horse models and My Little Ponies in various little nooks and crannies around the homestead. Spring was muddy and wet, but that just meant there were streams in the back in which to splash. Fall was about picking apples and jumping in giant piles of leaves while anticipating the first snowflake. Winter was all about burrowing into the snow, sledding down the hills in the neighbor's pasture and skating on the frozen cow pond.

As a child, all I needed to be content was a warm place to sleep, my imagination, and enough time outside. I could be happy anywhere with a book, a blanket, family, and food to eat. I spent hours in my room or outside, just being with myself, imagining possibilities and daydreaming. I noticed the fluidity of life, and the importance of nature. There seemed to be endless possibility and potential. Agile and free, I didn't attach to outcomes. Life was exciting; every day was a new adventure just wanting to happen.

Many of us can identify with that feeling of childhood possibility and freedom, from those who grew up in city apartments to those who roamed the woods. Children seem to be able to find a sense of home in adults they trust, in routine, in the feeling of adventure. Resilient and adaptable, many young kids are comfortable with their dependence and lack of control.

As we age, so often we get sucked into the cultural story of lack and scarcity. Of course, lack and scarcity are part of too many stories in a world ripe with systems that aren't supportive of all people and groups equally. But even when we have what we need to survive, busyness or anxiety take the steering wheel on a regular basis, and we forget to notice the possibilities. Expectations and outcomes drive our perception of how life is going. Home changes as we age from a feeling of freedom to a feeling of stress. What once was light now feels heavy. What once was full of possibility now feels like a rut.

## OTHER VOICES

Catherine remodeled and insulated a 1970s-era RV and has been living in it since 2014. Her home is a thirty-foot solar-powered work of art named Gertie. One summer she painted giant orange, green, and turquoise butterflies on the exterior. She's lived everywhere from Taos to the Rockies to California. The view out her window is constantly changing, and Catherine finds her astonishment by embracing that change.

Ellie and I talk about this often. She told me that she intentionally avoided that rut for a long time. After graduating from high school, she lived in fifteen different places over the next several years. In that transient season of life, she got very good at building a sense of home quickly. She infused each place with good memories, good wine, good people, and good books. As a renter, she didn't pick out paint colors or think about long-term improvements.

Denver, New York City, and Uruguay all became home for Ellie. Moving to new neighborhoods regularly kept her eyes fresh and her spirit grateful. She loved wandering around, drinking in her surroundings. It kept the gratitude flowing. With a house never in the picture or on the horizon, her definition of home remained playful. Her body was her home. El Salvador, Kenya, and Minneapolis were home. A pitching mound, balance beam and yoga mat, her spouse and kids were all deeply home.

Then it came time to think about buying a house.

When thinking of the cliché American dream, most of us picture a house with a white picket fence. In our society, home ownership somehow says, "You've made it!" or "You are now a full-fledged citizen of the United States of America." It feels good to own a house, to be able to do what we want with the paint colors or front yard decor. It can be a good investment. However, once the glow of having control, investing wisely, and "making it" wears off, reality sets in. Home maintenance takes over the to-do list. Buyer's remorse is a real thing.

Ellie's story is a prime example of this: Even though she fought this thread of the American dream for years, it eventually came time to settle in one spot. Buying made the most sense. When it was time to take action and choose one, she was reluctant and resistant. She cried the day her offer was accepted. She felt overwhelmed and trapped. It felt permanent. She understood the financial advantages to owning; she and her spouse researched the decision responsibly. But she loved being a renter. She loved being mobile, deciding how much space she wanted for twelve months and then reassessing. She didn't want to think about the color of the walls or the length of the lawn. She didn't want to be house poor or spend her free time on home repair. Truly owning struck her as an illusion, especially on land taken from Indigenous people. She had to decide that she could maintain her values as a homeowner. She owns the house; the house doesn't own her. The house did not need to eclipse her sense of home but could add to it. It could provide a space to entertain, a space to garden, a space to take root. What if she lost her sense of astonished gratitude in routine and a mortgage? When she signed on the dotted line, she was underestimating the astonishing power of seed planting and taking root.

While Ellie begrudgingly looked for houses in Minneapolis, my family and I moved into a little red house well outside of the metro area. I loved the close proximity of natural areas, lakes, and the space for gardening. The house was the right size for a family of three, perched in between two ravines, overlooking a small lake. I could imagine my daughter growing up enchanted with the natural world, looking for fairies and nymphs in the surrounding woodlands.

I don't regret our decision to take out a mortgage and commit to fixing the place up. Yet, much like Ellie, at times I have mixed feelings about the realities of homeownership as a white middle class person in America. I think about the people who lived where I do now, hundreds of years ago, before the area was colonized. Who were they? What did they dream of and celebrate? What delighted them? How can I live in this house and honor their memory in a respectful way? What is my role in reparations toward the marginalized groups of people who are their great-great-grandchildren? Not to mention the everyday realities of always having something to fix and being responsible for fixing it. We so often end up spending time and money on urgent home repair instead of traveling or donating to good causes. Home ownership is a complicated thing.

I want my house to be full of light. I want to feel abundantly satisfied, filled up with goodness and authenticity. When I come inside at the end of the day, I want to feel cozy and content and embraced by the space. A lot of us want something similar. So how do we create a sense of home in our dwellings? How can our houses facilitate living each day grounded in gratitude for what is, instead of fear of lack or worry or guilt? How can we return to the sense of freedom, gratitude, and potential we may have had as children in the homes our parents created? If we didn't have a sense of freedom and gratitude as children, how can we create that now, from scratch?

### OTHER VOICES

Kate and Eduardo bought a duplex with their friends to create a mini-intentional community. The two families, with four children between them, created semi-permeable boundaries between the two spaces. They eat dinner together four nights a week, share house upkeep responsibilities, and look after each other's children. The kids feel like close cousins, and the parents acknowledge that the arrangement helped fight the isolation often felt by young parents.

One summer day a few years after we'd moved into the little red house, we returned from a family vacation to a terrible smell and blaring alarm. A little creature had chewed through the cord that powered the septic pump, shorting it out. Another little critter was decomposing behind the fridge. We figured out how to fix those things, and then the water heater broke. An indoor cat got out and wouldn't come back in. Road construction out front kept interfering with the phone and internet lines, cutting modern communication for days at a time. A young black man was killed by police at a routine traffic stop in our old urban neighborhood. We found out the furnace needed to be replaced. The garage needed a new roof.

During those weeks, it seemed like there was more wrong than right.

As all of this was piling up, I realized I needed to do something other than just stew about what was wrong. I started writing in my gratitude journal, a practice I'd set aside when things got busy. Making time for it made a difference. Practicing gratitude for what was good, even alongside the unwanted and tragic, helped me appreciate moments that otherwise may have passed by, unnoticed.

The days the internet was down, I took more walks outside and noticed the pole beans starting to blossom. I spent more time in the garden and dug three colors of potatoes, picked kale, and found a baseball-bat-sized zucchini. I ate three perfectly ripe Sungold tomatoes directly off the vine, their sweetness exploding in my mouth like a sunset surprise in the western sky. After a hot run around road construction equipment, I ran through the garden hose with my squealing four-year-old daughter. We picked the blueberries that had turned over-ripe while we were away and discovered they were still plenty tasty. In the evenings (no internet, remember?), I listened to birds and frogs singing their melodies as dusk fell on the lake. It was a time of abundant astonishment, which I don't think I would have noticed had I not been intentional about voicing what was good.

There will always be hardship and challenge and things on the house that break. But there will also be ripe tomatoes, blueberry-stained fingers, the feel of a child's hand in mine, and the call of a loon through the darkness. No matter how hard things get, there will always be little delights to fill in the gaps with gratitude.

## OTHER VOICES

Susan didn't like how much time she and her husband were spending on house maintenance and improvement while her two boys were young. They sold their house and bought a small two-bedroom condo across from a park. The square footage makes it easy to clean and keep up and also encourages them to have outdoor time after school every day regardless of the weather. Downsizing has increased their happiness.

My friend Nancy is a jazz singer. After growing up in small-town Minnesota, she made her way to New York City to offer her gifts of music to the world. She spends some time in New York, but just as much time traveling, from China to Denmark to France to Minnesota. She gave up her apartment in the city and doesn't have a permanent address, choosing instead to stay with friends and family when needed. Sometimes the location changes as frequently as every few weeks. One August evening we were chatting when she was in Minnesota for an event. It came up that though she'd chosen this vagabond lifestyle, sometimes she'd felt adrift. She was occasionally frightened due to the unpredictability of her situation. Then on tour one summer, she woke up feeling deeply at home—in a small Texas town she'd never been to before. She said, "Just as I was waking up, before I had even opened my eyes, I had a strong sense of being home within myself, but I didn't remember where I was physically. I'm quite grateful for [that experience] as it's helped me to discover my own sense of 'home' that goes with me wherever I am." Her feelings of being adrift weren't tied to the place she lived, rather it was more of an internal awareness that she had felt much of her life, something unnamed until it wasn't. The physical exploration of a more transient lifestyle helped her find her internal home since she didn't have the distraction of naming a physical place as "home." She found that sense of home within, deep in her core. No matter where she goes, she carries that sense of gratitude, that sense of home, with her.

Intentionally acknowledging those things for which we are grateful in our current lives, especially those things that may surprise us, can create the foundation to live from a place of spaciousness. We can build a sense of grateful astonishment in the house or apartment or body that is our home. We can reclaim the capacity to be ok with impermanence and struggle. We can look for beauty and cultivate room within ourselves for imagining possibility while still loving and living in the present. When we find little bits of good even in the midst of challenge, we grow strong roots.

### OTHER VOICES

Josh's analytical brain loves numbers and logic. His family lived in a suburb south of the city. Since both Josh and his wife had a sizeable commute north to work every day, Josh figured out how much money they would save annually by moving north, a few suburbs closer to the city. The number, including gas, time as money, and wear on the car, was so much bigger than he expected that they put their house up for sale almost immediately and are much happier with shorter commutes.

What if our gratitude came from the assumption that there could have been nothing? Each one of us is an astonishment of cells that have come together in a unique way—we could have never been, but here we are, and there is love, kindness, and beauty all around if we dare look for it. Even if we have to peer around unwanted roadblocks or through a grimy windshield. When we are in touch with gratitude, we embody a sense of home.

As we put down roots, whether in a house we buy or in our hearts, our roots widen, reaching deeper into the earth to sustain and renew. In that way, we're like trees. Limbs get stronger as we raise babies or care for aging parents, lifting, rocking, squatting, embracing, lowering. Transient or not, there is a purpose in stillness, giving light, shade, and presence. The winds may cause us to bend, but they don't have to break us. All humans have the capacity for calm, peace, and joy to be at the center. Ellie told me about a time she was sitting on a blanket in the backyard with her boys, reading books, listening to birds and exploring toys. They stopped for every single plane that flew overhead. Delight lit them up. She watched too, with them, one on her lap and the other's hand on her leg. They got curious about who was in those planes, where they were coming from, and where they were going. They wished the travelers well and then got back to the business of playing. Maybe that is the spirit of gratitude and astonishment that everyone would do well to own— always getting back to the business of exploring our delight.

A few times a year I go back to visit my folks at my childhood home in South Dakota, that place where I learned to imagine. The prairie always helps me reset and reclaim my center. The land reminds me how to be alive, how to pay attention, how to see beauty in the ordinary, in the fleeting. The open space, the wide blue sky, and the endless sea of grass leave room for possibility, for good things to happen, for buds to open, for the imagined to take on a new life. It will always offer a sense of home.

The wooden walls that my parents built seem to absorb, hold on, and remember. They have witnessed and weathered herds of kids, mud, soccer balls, and flying vegetables. The walls speak of the deep roots that tie my family together with memory, the roots that form a vast web beneath the surface and hold the soil in place. Being there on that prairie homestead always invites me back to gratitude. It offers a lens of abundance, a sense of expansion.

Practicing and leaning into gratitude helps us embrace whatever comes next, and to imagine the possibilities that are always on the horizon no matter how many things seem to be going wrong. Gratitude helps us recognize that home is more than a building, or a town, or a country. Home is a feeling that lives inside us.

A seed is a tiny thing that can always be planted, even when weather conditions seem tenuous, the soil is rocky, and the length of the growing season is unknown. It's been said that to plant a seed is to believe in tomorrow. Keep planting seeds. Say hello to a stranger. Start a flower garden or plant lettuce seeds. Be astonished by what happens as a result. With that gratitude we hold the key to being home, no matter where we are.

### ᙏᙇᙇ THE TINY THING ᙇᙇᙇ
## An invitation to gratitude

For the great open secret is this: gratitude is not dependent on our external circumstances.[1]

–JOANNA MACY

Write down three things for which you are grateful. It's
true that "gratitude" seems to grace every book about
personal development, but what if you allowed yourself to be surprised by what you uncover? Get yourself a
nice leather journal, a cheap composition notebook, or
a pad of Post-its to act as a depository for your bits of
astonishment—your little seeds of goodness. Keep it by
your bedside, along with a writing utensil. At the end of
the day, just as you are readying yourself for sleep, reflect
on the day. Hone in on three things during the last 24
hours that were remarkable and write them down. What
delighted or astonished you? They can be little things,
like the feeling of sunlight on your shoulders or the
sound of laughter in your home. A kind word from a
neighbor. How the food gets from a farm field to your
fridge. You might write a whole page, full of descriptions
and illustrations and praise for the good in your life. Or

1. Joanna Macy and Molly Young Brown, *Coming Back to Life* (Gabriola
Island: New Society Publishers, 2014).

you might write three words. You are breathing. You have made it through another day. And at the end of the day, sometimes it's enough to write, "I am alive."

## Body Practice

Once a day, if it's accessible for you, lay on the ground with your feet up the wall [an alternative might be to recline on your bed with your knees up]. Splay your arms out wide. Notice how reversing gravity on your feet brings relief. Notice the floor and the wall supporting you. Allow your body to surrender to the earth and relax. After a few minutes, rise, refreshed from a few moments looking with a new perspective.

## In Reflection

* What about your home overwhelms you? How do you get stuck in negativity?
* What represents the idea of "home" for you?
* What are you grateful for in regard to home? Your life in general?
* How does it feel to notice the good?
* What makes you gasp in astonishment? And what helps you to notice these things?

* What patterns stand out as you name what's right and good in your life?
* What changes when you look through a lens of gratitude?
* What sort of seeds are important for you to plant?
* What seeds do you want to plant more of?
* What is another tiny thing that could work to cultivate gratitude in your life?

# Sensuality

sen·su·al·i·ty
\sen(t)SHəˈwalədē\
*noun*

the enjoyment, expression, or pursuit of physical, especially sexual, pleasure

Allow your body to take up space by wanting
what it wants.

## Ellie

As a child, I learned the unwritten rules around being a girl. Use your voice, but don't speak too loudly. Tend to your looks, but make it look like you don't. Stand out, but not too much. Know what you want, but don't ask for it directly. The margin of error seemed cruel. If your skirt was too short you were too sexual. If it was too long you were not sexual enough. How much space could I take up? We were rewarded for finding the line and not crossing it. It calls to mind a memory I have of watching my mom color a tree in one of my coloring books.

After my afternoon nap, my mom took the "Strawberry Shortcake" coloring book and the 64 pack of Crayola Crayons out of the craft cupboard. She got the supplies because she didn't like when I get fingerprints on the wood around the knobs. My mom sat next to me on the long wooden bench and scooted us closer to the table. I swung my legs around to sit on my heels so I could see the pages better. The vinyl tablecloth was navy and red plaid to match the wallpaper. She opened the coloring book to an untouched page and ran her pointer finger over the tips of the crayons, deciding on her first color.

I thought my mom was the best colorer in the whole world. When she colored a tree, she started with just the right shade of green—Shamrock—and followed the black outlines with a steady, thick line. Then she took three different greens—Inchworm, Fern, and Asparagus—and lightly shaded the tree in, blending the colors just so. You couldn't see where one stopped and another started. Just when I thought she was finished with the leaves, she took Lemon and added light touches. The tree shined against the gray of the paper. She never colored a tree purple. She never colored outside the lines. This careful precision and control were part of what I equated with femininity. She knew how to follow the rules handed to you, stay inside the lines and make something beautiful. I wanted to be just like my mom.

**OTHER VOICES**

Melissa takes up space best by dancing. Moving her body how it wants to move has helped her tap into who she is and what she most desires. She taps into her intuitive nature and releases any judgments about herself or other people. Dancing allows her to live rooted in the unexpected, acting in ways that make her feel what she wants to feel.

As I grew, however, I experienced staying inside the lines as limiting. In that place, I felt out of touch with my desires. I was drawn to women who take up space, who cross lines and boundaries with abandon, who know what they want and get it unabashedly. Take, for example, my friend Jennie from graduate school. I would always gaze at her, amazed. She was covered in tattoos and piercings. Her clothes didn't match.

Her hair was asymmetrical. Her gender, her sensuality, her voice, her smell, her thighs—they all took up space. She talked with her mouth full of food and said what she meant. She didn't shave her armpits and kissed who she wanted. She stayed out late and slept in and never dreamt of apologizing for something she didn't do. She was an avid biker living in New York City. I adored her then, and I adore her now. Just by being in the world, she challenged me to stop hiding.

Yoga helped. I started in a Thursday evening Vinyasa II class. It often filled up quickly. The sounds of the heat hissing through the vents and bare feet delicately moving around unrolling mats added to the hush. The instructor started the class with everyone in child's pose. It's a good place to start. She conducted the synching of breath in the room. Looking around, she noticed trapezoid muscles and the curves of shoulder blades, hair textures and hand ligaments. The bodies were beautiful, including mine, each in their own way. Even in a pose of surrender, our skin started to glisten with sweat from the swelling heat. She stepped carefully, barely able to maneuver between the situated mats.

"Welcome to your mat," she offered. "Extend your limbs to use every inch of it throughout class today. Send your spirit, your energy out into the world with every breath. Take up space. Let's begin."

Yoga is just one example of a corrective to the societal hum telling us to play small. The mat is a tangible boundary that challenges us to take up more space with our bodies in a way that feels powerful and beautiful, supple and strong. The mat connects us to the earth, and grounds us in our humanity, while we reach toward the sky. We can sit in the tension of our simultaneous smallness and vastness.

Biking helped, too. I didn't have a car in New York City, and biked everywhere. I have an embodied memory of biking south down a busy urban boulevard—the wind, the sun, the traffic, the city instantly got endorphins moving through my veins. I felt strong on my bike, getting somewhere on my own power. The street had a bike lane, but I liked that double-parked cars and delivery trucks full of butchered animals or cases of beer forced me to veer into traffic. I deserved to be there, too. There was a little dance on the street that was dynamic, a pact that passes between drivers, walkers, and bikers. No one wanted to hurt or be hurt. It made me feel alive. I could check over my left shoulder, put my hand out, and merge into traffic to turn left at a green light. The car behind me would always slow a bit to give me space. Every time, it felt like a little victory that's all mine.

Some folks feel more comfortable playing it small. We have been taught as children to color inside the lines. While we are going through puberty, we are led to believe that if our pants are too tight, we are the wrong size, not the pants. We are rewarded for finding the minuscule line between blending in and standing out, between docile and demanding. We want to be small, and we want to feel worthy of the space we take up. And so often we just don't know what we really want at all.

When I bring up my struggle to take up space in the world, Heidi gives me a knowing smile. She is a quiet, thoughtful person who treads lightly on the earth. She once told me a story about a summer hike in the Rocky Mountains with four other camp staff members. After plodding through snow drifts and ice-covered ledges, they made it to a gorgeous alpine lake. It was perfectly calm, full of shimmering water and welcoming sunlight. One of the women stood up, shed her hiking clothes, gave the group a sly grin and walked into the icy water.

### OTHER VOICES

Julie married into Egyptian culture, a culture that is highly sensual. It is a country full of intricate designs, scents, and tastes that delight, music and sounds that speak to the soul. People speak, argue, and laugh loudly. In their grief, wailing is encouraged. She started purchasing indulgent lotions, scents, and fabrics. She pampers, embraces, and nurtures her changing body.

Skin pale after a long midwestern winter, and feeling out of shape, Heidi hesitated. She didn't want to be seen. She shied away from boldly taking up space.

A shirt flew through her peripheral vision as one of the guys ran into the water. The sun was warm, and the water looked so inviting she felt courage rising in her. Her body woke up to what it wanted, the cool water against her skin. Wanting to shed her fears and limitations, she threw off her clothes and dived in. The feeling of crisp water took her breath away for a moment, and she felt truly alive.

Later, drying off on the rocks, she took up all the space she needed. The world is sustained by words and stories, yes, but also holy gasps.

Our minds override our bodies, telling us we are too pale and too doughy to strip down and go skinny-dipping in an alpine lake, even if it's what our bodies desperately want. If we can allow our bodies to reign now and again, we could find ourselves drying off in the decadent warmth of the rocks, laughing with friends. We could become more ourselves by really living embodied lives.

Being willing to take up literal and figurative space has been a growing edge for me. Coloring inside the lines soothes me. I like to feel contained. I like to play by the rules. The older I got, the better I got at following the rules: A gymnast's body is supposed to be compact. A woman's voice is supposed to be tempered. A lady's legs are supposed to be crossed. The rules are set up for women to play small and disappear. So, I must be willing to break the rules, push the boundaries, color outside the lines and take up more space to be true to my person. The world needs our full personhood, our boldness, not our hiding.

Being in touch with my sensuality is about recognizing that beyond needs, I also have desires. These desires are normal, healthy, life-giving, and beautiful. Honoring my desires, tending to my person takes courage. It feels vulnerable to express and enjoy pleasure. I have to convince myself that the pursuit of pleasure is not a self-serving waste of time. Practicing my sensuality is a necessary, revolutionary act.

### OTHER VOICES

Laura's trips to New York City reminded her of what it felt like to spend her time exactly how she wanted. Could she bring this freedom to her everyday life? Instead of making plans, she started acting from a true desire. She went outside and exercised alone or connected with friends or took a nap. She calls them intuitively guided days.

Naming our sexual desire as women and non-binary folks can also be uncommon. I facilitate conversation around sexual pleasure and healthy intimacy with youth and young adults. Girls and women often share with me that these topics do not come up in their lives. They didn't for me when I was a girl and a young woman. We need permission to explore sexual desire. Navigating my sexuality in isolation was challenging at best, and painful at times, too. My friend group kept our feelings, thoughts, concerns, questions, and experiences around pleasure a secret. We also hid times we were harassed and assaulted even though we shared everything else about our lives. Now, I love normalizing meaningful conversation around sexual desire and claiming sexual pleasure. There are more and more wonderful books and podcasts, too, to accompany us into the physical, spiritual, mental, emotional, and sexual health that leads to thriving and wholeness.

My personality type wires me to easily put others' needs before my own, and societal gender pressure exudes that instinct. Strategic correctives like biking and yoga help. I choose a partner and friends who understand this about me and invite me to bring my personhood to the relationship. My spouse has been gentle with me as I explore my desires around food and bodies. In his presence, I can let my body want what it wants.

Sometimes my body wants slightly bizarre things, like lying flat on the hardwood floor while he presses the heel of his hand down onto my sternum. It creeps him out a little, to straddle me and bear down on my breastbone. But he sees the relief it brings me and has come to trust that my skeleton is strong. The pressure releases something locked inside. I close my eyes, exhale, and feel the back of my ribs curl up slightly as if they were smiling. Warmth spreads over my chest.

After a minute or so I whisper, "Okay, thank you."

He gently removes his hand and usually leans down and kisses me before helping me up to standing. I am unstuck. I can breathe. Lighter, liberated, I proceed with my day.

Sometimes, my spouse anticipates what my body wants even before I do. I think of the time he walked in from the kitchen with a Clementine orange in his hand. He sat next to me on the couch and leaned forward to place his elbows on his knees. Deliberately, he peeled the Clementine so that the rind stayed in one piece. The peel landed on the coffee table, spread out so it looked like a starfish. Without turning, he passed me a portion of the Clementine. I hadn't asked for it. I smiled at the back of his head, grateful. As he sat back to rest his head next to mine on the back of the couch, he passed me one more segment, so we had equal parts. He did it absentmindedly, without ceremony. Before I ate it, I lined the single piece up against the larger section, making a perfect half. These small moments of sensuality between me and my spouse add up over my days and creates a playground for me to come in touch with my desires.

In our exploration of sensuality, Heidi decided to start asking her body what it truly wants in the morning, when she could hear it whispering in the quiet. After drinking coffee first thing in the morning for years, it had become her default. But when she brought some intentionality to her morning routine, she discovered her body really wanted water first thing. Room temperature. With her morning thirst quenched, her body responded with gentle gratitude.

How do our bodies yearn for nourishment? For refreshment? Do they want to slip into ice cold water on a sun-drenched day high in the mountains? Do they want some yoga or biking? How do our bodies want to exist in partnership with other bodies? How do they want to be autonomous? What does it mean for our bodies to take up space in a way that feels right and good and that doesn't apologize for things?

We are social creatures who crave intimacy. More than just bodily arousal, we long for a gentle caress of the cheek, a person to cry with, a conversation about the black holes, life and death, and immigration reform. Practicing sensuality is acknowledging our human need for intimacy and pursuing it joyfully. Rooted in self and reaching toward pleasure, our beings take up space with ease and grace, enjoying the moment wholeheartedly. When we can tap into what truly satisfies desire, and when we can give into the vulnerability that comes along with that, we're taking up space in a way that serves our needs, and consequently, the needs of those we love.

## ᗯᕈᖇ THE TINY THING ᖇᕈᗯ
### An invitation to desire

We know we must decide whether to stay small, quiet, and uncomplicated or allow ourselves to grow as big, loud, and complex as we were made to be.[1]

–GLENNON DOYLE

Take a few moments in the morning and decide what you really want to drink as the first thing. Close your eyes. Listen to your body. Let yourself want what you want. Take as much time as you need to really identify your desire, then mindfully prepare and consume it. As you drink, notice how your body responds. Is it indeed what you wanted? How is it nourishing you?

Sensuality is all about claiming, embracing, naming and celebrating what your animal body really wants. First thing in the morning, our self-consciousness is quiet, and we can tap into what our body is wanting. Notice where the desire unfolds from in your body. Notice how gently and clearly it tells the truth if you take the time to listen. It may take courage to state a true desire and fulfill that desire.

---

1. Glennon Doyle (Melton), *Love Warrior* (New York: Flatiron Books, 2017).

This simple, mindful choice and consumption can set the tone for your entire day. Move toward the good stuff—soulful music, rich wine, meaningful touch, needed rest. Your being uses your body to communicate. Your body is smart, and it knows how to take care of you, how to nourish you and how to heal itself. Simplicity is not about self-deprecation but living out of a true sense of self. Choosing what your animal body really desires validates the self. It feels decadent and brings dignity. Your human desire is not something to shy away from, but to lean into and respond to with confidence and joy.

## Body Practice

Pick a part of your body that you either ignore or have negative feelings around and once a day show that part of your body physical affection. You can use lotion, oil, or simply your own warm touch.

## In Reflection

* In what ways have you been conditioned to not take up too much space?
* Whose needs do you put before your own? How?
* How does your body let you know what it wants?

* Which forms of intimacy—physical, mental, emotional, spiritual, sexual—come naturally to you?
* Who in your life provides intimacy—a safe space to explore your desires?
* What are your favorite ways to pursue pleasure?
* How can you build the practice of honoring your desires into your daily routine?
* What is another tiny thing that could cultivate sensuality in your life?

# Creativity

cre·a·tiv·i·ty
\ ˌkrēāˈtivədē\
*noun*

the use of the imagination or original ideas

Just start. Remember how it feels to create.

## Heidi

There is a myth surrounding how creatives live and work. I am a writer. So is Ellie, and she agreed that the myth goes something like this:

I rise in the morning, when the light slants in through the blinds, and walk down the steps to my home office. I switch on the lamp that sits atop the writing desk. Coffee brews upstairs. An open window lets in the breeze off the lake. After lighting a candle and stepping onto a well-worn yoga mat, I breathe deeply into my lower abdomen, reach my arms up to the ceiling, and move through a series of sun salutations. Half an hour goes by flowing through the postures that have become old friends over the years. Tipping my head forward, chin to chest, I set an intention for the day, say namaste, and blow out the candle. I roll up my yoga mat, pour a first cup of coffee, settle into my desk chair, pull up a word document, and start typing.

## OTHER VOICES

Iris treats her creative practice like a lover. She puts on yummy clothing, makes a delicious beverage, burns some palo Santo (wood from a South American tree used for healing), puts on a favorite CD, and loses herself in her project. When she feels an idea growing, she turns to nature so it will grow roots. She follows what excites her— the way the light hits a tree or how the forest smells on a morning walk. When she properly prepares and gives her creative practice time and attention, she can write a week's worth of content in a day.

When the flow stops, I look out the window at the lake and get invigorated. Inspirational items surround me— some favorite magazines, a photograph of a cherished alpine lake, a rock I picked up in Malta, a stack of books by Wendell Berry, and a gratitude journal.

Mid-morning, I go upstairs to fetch another cup of coffee and a scone, relax for a while with some light reading and then head back down to continue working. I take lunch just after noon, go out for an hour hike in the woods and resume writing until four. I then venture out to a local cafe to see people, tend the garden, or pick up some extra vegetables at the farmer's market. I prepare a nice dinner, enjoy it with my family, and spend the evening hours reading on the deck, listening to the frogs sing their lullabies.

If this day happens at all, it happens for a lucky few. For most of us, this day can be a crushing myth, an unattainable mark. We hold full-time jobs, hopefully with benefits. We raise children who are lovely and needy, urgent and messy. We have leaves to rake, meetings to attend, meals to drop off to sick friends, and toilets to clean. Yet creativity lurks, begging to be actualized, so we do the next best thing. We write in the margins.

I've written entire books between appointments at work, in my head while commuting or chopping vegetables. Ellie told me that when her kids were really young, she would write in the parked car while they slept in car seats. She also often writes on cocktail napkins and Post-it notes, any little bit of a surface that can absorb some words for safekeeping. Some of my other writer friends get up at 5:00 a.m. and write until their kids wake up. To be creative, we get creative. We squeeze it in. We dictate into our phones while running errands. We skip naps, showers, and leisurely Saturdays, weaving the writing into the fabric of our everyday lives. We try to write the truth in stolen moments. It can feel desperate and necessary.

But even while it can feel desperate and necessary, it is really hard to begin. For many of us, the barrier to creativity is starting. We say we want to write or paint, but we are reluctant to open a document or prepare a fresh canvas. Maybe the blank space is the start that we need. It sits there as a fresh beginning, and its existence may invite us to start creating on it. The empty document, the blank canvas, is our margin, the room we need to start chipping away at something new.

Creating requires loyalty to the inner self away from the interruptions of ordinary life. Artists gravitate toward the margins where there is space available to form something new. Women have always been in the business of creating something out of nothing—growing and nurturing life in our bodies, assembling food for our families—we have creativity in our bones and muscle fibers, passed on from our ancestors, waiting to be awakened. Ellie shared with me that when she was pregnant with her first son, she needed more and more time and space to prepare for his arrival and the shift in her life as her body took up more and more space in the world. I could relate—when I was pregnant with my daughter, I spent more time than ever before just pondering and writing and musing in quiet spaces. Our bodies were busy creating. Aware that what was happening was in no way ordinary, we wandered toward the margins to get quiet time, time to wonder and read and write. Time to pray and stretch and listen. Time to get to know the baby inside. During pregnancy, there is something profound happening, and we wanted to be present to it. Becoming a parent is far from the only example of transformation that requires space to create. Leadership requires space, as does teaching, building, community organizing, learning, and ministry. We may wander to open space in times of grief, crisis, romance, illness, and transition. We needed time on the margins of life to honor what was happening and let it transform us into the people we were becoming.

Gloria Steinem, in *My Life on the Road*, writes:

> I wish I could imitate the Chinese women letter writers of at least a thousand years ago. Because they were forbidden to go to school like their brothers, they invented their own script—called nushu or "women's writing"—though the punishment for creating a secret language was death. They wrote underground letters and poems of friendship to each other, quite consciously protesting the restrictions of their lives.

As one wrote, "Men leave home to brave a life in the outside world. But we women are no less courageous. We can create a language they cannot understand."[1]

Art tends to come to us from the margins. Interesting people reside on the margins. Interesting things are happening there. There is a counterculture offering a prophetic voice to the status quo and hypnotic current of the mainstream. Art breaks us from routine, interrupts our rote existence, invites us to a higher mind, infuses our lives with beauty, speaks truth to power.

Creating is about telling the truth. As humans, we want to understand ourselves, and creating can put us on that path. We need to have a voice, to feel visible, to use stories to make sense of the nonsensical moments. We desire to belong. We desire to grow. These are not just desires of an artist, but desires of humans. We are all creatives.

In 1929, Virginia Woolf wrote an extended essay that argued for a literal and figurative space for women writers in a literary tradition dominated by men. The essay is titled "A Room of One's Own." Today, the excavation work of creating space for women (or anyone in a caregiving role) is still exhaustingly real. Without intentional and constant

---

1. Gloria Steinem, *My Life on the Road* (New York: Penguin Random House, 2015).

upkeep, space can dissolve in a matter of moments. Creative workspaces get filled with diapers and Christmas wrappings, toys and bills, commuting and dinner prep. Time carved out to create disappears to sick children and errands to run and dishes to do. Yet taking time to carve out space in order to create, and tending to that space, benefits us all. A space to create is not a given and is rarely easily available. The work of digging out literal and figurative space to create, however, is always worth it.

## OTHER VOICES

Lisa left a war-torn country and a violent marriage to unite with her child in the United States. A writer, she felt pressure to be productive. She went weeks without writing anything. Finally, she stepped away from her computer and started writing in her journal about shame. She wrote until the shame was gone. "You can't force creativity," she says. "It has to flow."

Traveling to the margins requires an intentional commitment to actively move away from the mundane and dwell in the borderlands for a while. Yet getting to the margins is often not enough.

The work of maintaining and widening the margins, creating more space and actually dwelling there, is an ongoing swim upstream. It is an effort that is easy to give up on. We give in and settle into the gray lulling us into submission. We get used to what is already there and forget to dream about what could be. We accept the mundane or refuse to see the beauty that resides in ordinary life circumstances. So often it feels like any time commitment also requires the creation of something earth-shattering. Sometimes I clearly see the margins, but don't venture there until the conditions are perfect, and I don't think I'm alone in such a phenomenon. The land of creativity starts to feel intimidating or superfluous or out of reach. When life gets busy, I'm apt to forget that art is as essential as doing the laundry. Whenever we find resistance, it's a call to pay attention. There is something on the other side calling to us.

Ellie reminded me of Mary Oliver's, "Of Power and Time," which makes a distinction between the ordinary self and the creative self. So often fully-immersed in the act of everyday survival, we forget that we are also artists, whose job is to move the world forward. This requires a different mindset that is not ordinary, but extraordinary:

> Creative work needs solitude. It needs concentration, without interruptions. It needs the whole sky to fly in, and no eye watching until it comes to that certainty which it aspires to, but does not necessarily have at once. Privacy, then. A place apart—to pace, to chew

pencils, to scribble and erase and scribble again. . . . Certainly there is within each of us a self that is neither a child, nor a servant of the hours. It is a third self, occasional in some of us, tyrant in others. This self is out of love with the ordinary; it is out of love with time. It has a hunger for eternity. . . . And no artist could go about this work, or would want to, with less than extraordinary energy and concentration. The extraordinary is what art is about.[2]

When we embrace the margins instead of the myth of needing the perfect conditions to create, we can find the courage to start.

I set out a bowl and some measuring cups and open the cabinet door that hides the baking supplies. After creaming butter with sugar, I add a few eggs. Next come the flour and baking soda. Wielding a big wooden spoon, I stir until a sticky dough forms and pulls away from the sides of the bowl. Last, I add some chocolate chips. As the oven heats up, I drop one ball of dough at a time onto the prepared cookie sheet. My hands know this rhythm. I remember how it feels to create.

---

2. Mary Oliver, *Blue Pastures* (New York: Harcourt, 1995).

So many days, weeks, or even months in the life of a creative person are frustrating. Maybe you can relate. I wait for ideas to expand, for inspiration to find the poetry in the mundane, for the patience to keep working on tedious or daunting projects that feel like they will always be first drafts. I wait for responses to submissions, for reviews, for approval, for good sales. I let other people dictate my happiness. It's easy to give power to things I don't have control over, holding on tight to things that want to stay slippery. I put my contentment under condition, my very *creativity* under condition. So many of us stop carving out time to create things we love if it is not our profession. We say that things will be better once we hear from the editor, once the piece is purchased, once we have more time to create, once we figure out how to work self-care into our practice. It can feel desperate.

Creating takes courage and audacity. It takes seeing and claiming the margins as our own. When we do give into self-doubt, forget that we were born to create, or let others dictate our worth as creatives, we give away the power to live rooted in our own truth. Creativity, and the process that brings it about, is telling the truth in a way that feels right, no matter what it looks like and even if it feels like it's on stolen time. We keep creating in the margins. We keep telling the truth.

When I go out to the garden each spring, the ground is a mess of old grass, mud, and last year's squash vines.

Brandishing an old garden hoe, I start removing old plants and any weeds that got left from the last growing season. As the soil loosens up, I kneel on the freshly turned-over earth to make a shallow row and drop some peas into their new home. I cover them up and do it again. And again. An hour later, there is a patch of black earth marked with little sticks of promise. I remember how it feels to create.

## OTHER VOICES

Siri, known as Humbird in the music world, tells young creatives to keep a notebook with them at all times so they can capture ideas. Second, practice all the time so when you do have an idea you are skilled enough to execute it. And finally, maybe most importantly, finish things. "It's easy to start things, but artists finish things, too. That creates room and energy to keep creating."

Many creative folks talk about the fear of being dried up. Once we've created something, we wonder if we will ever create anything else ever again. No matter how long we are at it, we feel like imposters. We don't trust the creative process which includes times of quiet, rest, and incubation. We doubt. We think there is nothing left to share, convinced our avenues of speaking without using our voices are all permanently silenced. Then, either because we are rested or out of sheer willpower or because we are better people when we are creative, we find the audacity to start again. After all, we are a species that continually seeks meaning and purpose, and creating helps us on that journey.

My daughter and I sometimes camp out in front of the wood stove, her with a coloring book and me with an old sketchbook. Our colored pencils are between us so we can share. She concentrates, intent on getting more precise with her swaths of color. I hesitate, wondering if I'll remember how to draw this or that since it's been a long time since I've opened this sketchbook. It's been a long time since I've held a pencil in this way. Yet color fills the pages, lines are drawn, and I remember how it feels to create.

Our creative self is whispering, "Simply begin." It is asking us to push past the doubts we have about our capability to make something of worth and just make something. We can embrace the margins and create something from nothing. It may require claiming ten minutes between a run and a shower to write a few sentences. Or grabbing five minutes while the soup simmers to draw a line or two. This way, we can continue to weave creation into our days. By starting, we have made something. We have created, and in order to create anything, creativity comes into play. There's no deadline for exercising creativity—there is only a continual opportunity to begin and begin again.

Showing up is a sign of good faith that creativity will reward. We will become the vessels that the muses use to seep beauty and truth into the universe. Creating itself is transformative. The size and scope of the product does not matter. We have an opportunity to be extraordinary every day, but we must believe in our ability to engage in art one moment at a time. We cannot wait for a huge swath of time or for the light to be coming in through the window at just the right angle. We must grab and steal and snatch and cobble together our chances at creativity. It will look more mundane than we imagined. Drawing with our children, baking a cake, dancing in our living rooms, finger painting, watching an amazing film, taking a photograph, or adding to a scrapbook can add not only beauty and goodness to the world but change our eyes, minds, and hearts. It may not be especially beautiful or comfortable or emotional. The product will most likely be far from perfect, reflecting back at us our own messy humanity. But there is something in the discomfort, the awkward stumbling through, the functionality of the ritual that carries a beauty of its own.

Our ability to create something out of nothing or transforming something into something else is worthy of our awe. Engaging in creativity renews our sense of personhood, alters our perspective, and helps us get in touch with the profound nature of ourselves. Creating adds dignity and value to our time and place, to our lives and communities.

Just start. Remember how it feels to create. We'll meet at the margins. Beauty awaits us there.

---

### ꝏꝏꝏ THE TINY THING ꝏꝏꝏ
### An invitation to start

Make an empty space in any corner of your mind, and creativity will instantly fill it.[3]

–DEE HOCK

Start. That is to say, put your pencil to the paper and make one mark. Set the mixing bowl on the counter. Just set it there. Get your guitar out of the closet and place it in the living room. Turn the stereo on low and sway your body to the music. Dig your knitting needles out of the basket in the back bedroom and put them next to the rocking chair. Grasp the yarn, hold the needles, and cast on. Every act of creativity is just one tiny action, followed by another and another until there is something new.

Like throwing a stone into a calm pool of water, starting changes the surface. Start making ripples. And ripples take on a life of their own.

---

3. Staff, Fast Company, "Dee Hock on Management" (Fast Company, September 8, 2017).

## Body Practice

Once a day, cup both hands gently over your heart. Acknowledge the gift of this day, this life. Slowly move your body to face all four cardinal directions, taking a deep breath in each position. Remember that your heart can hold in balance every facet of your being. There is art inside you and all around, at the intersection as well as the margins.

## In Reflection

* What words come to mind when you think of "creativity"?
* What makes you feel creative?
* How does starting a new project change the day?
* How can you tap into your creativity in the stuff of regular, daily life?
* When does self-doubt tend to creep into the picture in your life? What would happen if this doubt didn't exist?
* What shifts when you know all you have to do is draw one line, rather than paint the whole masterpiece in one sitting?
* Where do you see art in the ordinary world?
* What is another tiny thing that could work to cultivate creativity in your life?

# Learning

learn·ing

\ˈlərniNG\

*noun*

the acquisition of knowledge or skills through experience, study, or by being taught

❧

Playfully explore the edges of your mind, body and being.

### Ellie

Violet grew up in Kibera, Kenya, where secondary education is not free. Because many families there cannot afford to send their children to school, girls often get married and start families at a young age. Violet found Kibera Girls Soccer Academy (KGSA), a free secondary school for girls in the neighborhood. Intentional, visionary work had gone into building a space in the middle of the slum for girls to learn. The subversively counter-cultural and transformative energy was palpable at KGSA. In between classes, girls chatted easily, playing together and sharing lip gloss, excited to return to class. They were comfortable and safe. They were taking up space unapologetically. They felt free.

> **OTHER VOICES**
>
> Steph is the mother of four very active boys. She recently realized that supporting the boys' learning had slowed her own. So, she started piano lessons. She is falling back in love with a joy of her own childhood. Her piano practice time is her sacred time to get away, connect with herself, and relearn something she enjoys.

Violet started part way into the year and had to play catch up. "My first day was so exciting," she said. "Girls were sitting up straight, raising their hands to answer questions. The teachers knew so much and were taking us seriously as students. I didn't even know what biology was, but I was excited to learn."

Violet knew then what we often take for granted now—learning is inherently good and exciting. It brings dignity and is worth fighting for. Learning makes us better versions of ourselves. And part of learning is admitting what we don't already know. In order to deepen our knowledge and expand ourselves, we inevitably knock up against our limits of body, mind, and being. We can choose to embrace our limits and playfully experiment with them, or we can live smaller, safely within our boundaries, and risk becoming sedentary.

Babies learn about an object by trying to eat it. With all of their senses on high alert, the vigor and urgency they show trying to figure things out is inspiring. As they grow, young children show no self-consciousness about asking questions or being confused. It is their job to learn. Why, why, why rings out like a refrain as they figure out the world.

At some point, the unabashed learning seems to slow. We stop using all of our senses to keep digging. We ask fewer questions. We don't like feeling confused. We focus on things we are naturally good at. We learn things that will advance our careers and leave the rest in the periphery. Appearing in control trumps continual growth and improvement.

Learning is a risk. Engaging in learning is admitting that you have room to grow. You want to expand your body, mind, and being from its current state. Yet again, it is claiming that you want to take up more space in the universe.

Committing to continual improvement implies that you have not yet arrived. And the process of learning carries with it the option of failure.

We learn so much from failure. Kids are failing joyfully all the time! Yet our society does not allow much room for failure. Can we support our children in failing so they can become adults who love growing so much that they embrace failing as part of the journey? Can we create a safe space for children to sit in discomfort so they may gain a capacity for wonder and endurance for seeing themselves through to the other side? Can we show the same patience and kindness to ourselves that we offer to children? Can we model learning for our children with all the risk and growth involved?

What if we allowed children to invite us back into a space of pure curiosity? As a child, I wondered about how toasters worked and where the stars came from and how old I would be when I first felt old. I sat and wondered for hours in my room or while following the raindrops as they slipped down the car window.

Do you remember what it felt like to learn something as a child? I remember the first time I saw my shoelace poking through the loop. Before I grabbed it, I knew that when I pulled, the knot I had been working so hard to create would appear. I was filled with pride and joy, showing my mom and trying again and again. I remember learning to read. A volunteer at my school taught me a trick to read the word *are.* "This is a hard one," she said when I hesitated. "If you say the middle letter, then you know the word!"

In adolescence, I grabbed my ball and glove and did my pitching drills daily. While my fastball, change-up, and drop ball improved, I started working on my curveball. It required a new grip and adjustments in the arm circle, release, and lower body thrust. More than any other pitch, the curveball manipulated the mechanics of the body from the foundational motion my body knew so well. After trying and trying, tweaking and altering, it finally worked. I knew the ball would curve as soon as it left my hand. Right before it crossed the plate, the ball swerved sharply to the outside corner. "Yes! That was it," my coach encouraged. "Did you feel it?" I did.

---

**OTHER VOICES**

Fighting the urge to hibernate during the cold Minnesota winters, Matt has committed to learning something new each snowy season. Last year he took up swing dancing. This year he signed up for classical guitar lessons. "When it's miserable outside," he says, "why not take the time to expand your repertoire?"

---

One night I sat in tears at my kitchen table trying to understand geometry proofs. My dad sat with me and never found the words to help me see the logical steps I needed to prove the congruence of the triangles. He sent me to bed to rest. "You will get it," he assured me. Then, the very next day in class, it clicked. There was light. I saw it. From then on, when a proof sat in front of me, instead of getting anxious, I took a deep breath and dug in with playful curiosity.

The moments of success—when I learned a word or made a new pitch work—are so powerful in my memory that I tend to forget how many times I failed before I succeeded. As a child, I was so intent on learning that I did not even register the times it didn't work as failure. They were just necessary steps I was taking toward learning successfully. How does failure become about something other than a necessary step to learn? When does learning become tailored away from wonder and toward productivity?

Heidi and I agree that watching our kids learn is a great invitation to explore our own openness or resistance to failure and growth. Heidi remembers watching her daughter Eva run across the grass at full speed when she was young. She was wearing her ball gown and carrying a bunch of wildflowers. Heidi wanted to yell, "Slow down!" but managed to refrain. Eva stepped right in a hole and fell hard to the ground. She was up again in an instant, frustrated, but she reclaimed her bouquet and kept on going. She continued to trip in that hole over and over. But then came the day that she slowed down and hopped over it. She equipped herself. Knowing how to get up again is an important life skill to learn. We hone our resiliency skills when we get back up after falling. The capacity to recover quickly helps cultivate self-efficacy and grit. When we can get up after a fall, we have deepened our roots.

We want our children to question the status quo and think for themselves. We want them to be safe and have plenty of opportunity to do what makes them feel fully alive. And we want them to be able to develop autonomy that comes from working through tough and unfamiliar situations. To get there, they are going to have to fail at things sometimes. And it will help to have that failure modeled for them.

### OTHER VOICES

Playful learning at work keeps our sense of vocation alive. As a corporate coach, Leslie felt like she hit a plateau. She carved out a chunk of her budget to buy new books and a chunk of her calendar to read, go to seminars, and get more training. She integrates learning into her schedule and is experiencing new excitement.

I remember a high school classmate of mine asking our math teacher, "When are we ever going to need to know this in the real world?"

"This is the real world," she answered. "You may never use this exact math method, but you will need to use your brain. We are developing the sharpness of your brain. We do not only learn in order to be useful."

My humanities teacher used to say, "The truth is already inside of you. I am not here to teach you anything new, but to awaken the truth that is lying dormant inside of you."

My philosophy teacher said, "I do not have the answers, but I do have a nose for truth. It is not my job to give you knowledge but to sit with you and simply say, 'Look, the truth went that way. Let's go find it.'"

My high school learning happened in the days pre- "Ok, Alexa . . . ," where we can get quick answers to any number of topics. I never mistook learning for simply acquiring answers to questions and gaining knowledge of facts. I ultimately attached to the discipline of theology, I think, in part because it was filled with wonder and grappling. The more I learned the more interesting the subject became, but ultimately, I knew I would always arrive at a place where I experience my limits as a human creature with a limited human brain. At the end of the day, many questions about God, life, death, suffering, joy, love, and the universe end with us admitting that we just don't know. Learning, then, does not have a destination but is brimming with wonder. As we strive in the exercise of practicing theology, progress looks like asking more interesting questions and cultivating a mature curiosity. I came to know that disciplines like math and science end in wonder as well. Learning in all areas is an opening, a constant new beginning, a journey without a destination, driven by wonder and curiosity—a thirst that quick answers cannot quench.

The gift my high school teachers gave me was a varied sense of learning—learning to learn, learning a skill, learning for fun, learning for risk, for failure, for growth. They reminded me that learning is inherently good. We can create room to practice failing so that the sting of failure and its tie to shame is taken away. We can recognize the power of learning from failure. We can build playgrounds in our lives that we tend to, making it ripe for learning. There, we can courageously approach curiosity and failure with playfulness. There, we can lean into discomfort and confusion as an exciting opportunity to grow.

It was easy to keep my love of learning going in college and my young adult life. Teaching kept me learning with my students. I kept earning new degrees. I playfully took things up like marathon running. I'm bad at running long distances really, which is kind of refreshing. I get a lot out of running, and part of the growth for me is being okay with not improving. I run just to run, and even though I run slowly, I am very proud of my marathon finishes. I experience my limits and attempt to enjoy them.

I also took up yoga as an adult in part because the learning is new every day. There is no destination. The practice models the idea of humility, continual improvement, and curiosity of the self that I want to overflow into other areas of my life.

More recently, however, I catch myself slipping into stagnancy. I got busy doing only the things I'm good at. I learned things that forward my careers strategically, and I forgot to carve out time to learn just to learn. I avoided failure and discomfort. My curiosity atrophied; my wonder lulled to sleep. I took education for granted. I stopped playfully engaging with the limits of my body, mind, and being. I put my bucket list in a drawer and used my safe, established box of tools. I cultivated learning opportunities for my kids and called it a day instead of learning with them and modeling playful curiosity and engagement with failure.

I'm not alone in this. Heidi noticed the same thing in herself and decided to do something about it. Recently, Heidi sat down at an electric pottery wheel for the first time. She was surrounded by good potters and felt intimidated. She felt old. She almost got up and left. Instead, she mustered up the courage to put a small piece of clay on the wheel. She couldn't center the clay. After two hours, she felt defeated. Yet she returned week after week.

On the last day of class, sitting on the ware rack were several imperfect pieces Heidi had created. Showing up had felt scary and frustrating and embarrassing, but that's what learning is. Her failures were her steppingstones. Just like a potter's glaze, they add another layer to what makes it beautiful to be a human.

Life is best experienced through the lens of curiosity and joy. We all have weaknesses that we want to protect—but we also all have the capacity to build resiliency. We don't need to give up our curiosity to perfectionism. When we can allow ourselves the freedom to fall down so we can get back up again and thrive, we keep learning and deepening our roots in ways that nourish our branches. Every day we have a choice. We can risk. We can choose to grow, expand, improve. There is so much to learn.

～✎～ THE TINY THING ～✎～
An invitation to curiosity

Develop a passion for learning. If you do, you will never cease to grow.[1]

–ANTHONY J. D'ANGELO

Identify one thing you'd really like to learn. It could be a skill, a topic area, a person. Maybe the person you want to learn more about is yourself. Name what the first step will be in beginning to learn. Commit to taking that first step.

Life is hard. Our brains are tired. We tell ourselves that we have earned and deserve rest from learning,

---

1. Anthony J. D'Angelo. *The College Blue Book: A Few Thoughts, Reflections & Reminders on How to Get the Most Out of College & Life* (New York: Arkad Press, 1995).

improvement, and growth. True. Yet we owe it to ourselves to keep unfolding. Building learning back into our routine, even for fifteen minutes a day, can bring us back to life, awaken the imagination, and invite us back into active citizenship. Learning is inherently good. Tending to the mind can be relaxing and invigorating.

## Body Practice

Once a day, intentionally turn your hands so they are facing palms up. This can work sitting or standing, walking or still. Notice what shifts in your being with this slight change of posture. Do you feel open? Vulnerable? Curious? Can your hands invite your whole self to be open to newness and growth?

## In Reflection

* What is a memory you have from childhood learning?
* What did school teach you about learning?
* What is one of your experiences of failure that you can now consider a gift?
* When have you witnessed someone else experiencing the joy of learning?

* When was a time when confusion was uncomfortable for you?
* What is something that you have always wanted to
  learn?
* How might you lean into uncertainty the next time
  something feels new?
* What is another tiny thing that could work to cultivate curiosity in your life?

# Community

com·mu·ni·ty
\kəˈmyo͞onədē\
*noun*

a group of people living in the same place or having a
particular characteristic in common

In vulnerability, we find community.

## Heidi

In his *Vanity Fair* essay "The Bonds of Battle," Sebastian
Junger explores why soldiers miss war when it's over. With
danger and loss often comes closeness. War requires deep

vulnerability, creating a fertile ground for community. Soldiers eat and sleep together, move as a group, and make decisions collectively. They are never alone. Their individual survival depends on the group. They rely on each other completely. This mimics our hunter-gatherer ancestry, when humans needed cooperation and sharing, and evolutionarily, we still crave that.

Soldiers arrive home to a highly isolated existence comparatively, which can cause depression and a longing to return to war—not for the danger, but for the sense of community. There is no replacement for the closeness of war buddies or that highly intense sense of the common good. They go from close quarters and groupthink to a society where "most people work outside the home, children are educated by strangers, families are isolated from wider communities, personal gain almost completely eclipses collective good, and people sleep alone or with a partner."[1] Even civilians, Junger says, can get nostalgic for the crisis of war that unite people together.

We are social, dependent, interwoven creatures. Soldiers know that we must rely on each other to get through life because they have experienced how interdependence helps keep them alive. War is an extreme context to think about community, but Junger raises interesting and applicable points. When I think back to high school, cooperation,

---

1. Sebastian Junger, *Vanity Fair*, "The Bonds of Battle" (June 2015).

working toward a common good, loyalty, and close quarters come to mind. Growing up in a family of six, the house was always full of people. I spent the day with hundreds of classmates, the afternoons with cross country or gymnastics teammates, and the evenings with family. There were moments when I wished I had more friends or lamented not being invited to certain parties, but I was rarely alone. All around me, communities formed in theater, band, and choir rooms, on sports fields, and during study sessions. Groups of all sorts offered support and a shared sense of purpose.

## OTHER VOICES

Michelle and a few friends turned the house they rent into an intentional community. They have house meetings once a week, cook and eat together several nights a week, and host community events like fundraisers, book clubs and discussions. As renters move on, potential renters interview to join. During a life stage that can feel lonely, Michelle feels supported and fed.

Then in college, I had not just one but four assigned roommates, as well as classmates, teammates, and fellow band or club members. There were even a few familiar faces from high school to help fight the feelings of loneliness and isolation until new friend groups formed. Campus life offered built-in community.

College graduates can go through a rough transition. There are no longer dorms, cafeterias, classrooms, campus ministries, choirs, or Greek life offering the potential to grow community. What replaces things like competitive sports teams, clubs, and campus social events? All of a sudden, I was on my own in a strange city, spending each day with co-workers who didn't seem very interested in getting to know me. Living with two of my brothers near their university where they were soccer players, I witnessed their community form, even while I floundered with the abrupt shifts to my own social opportunities. The sudden lack of easy camaraderie was disorienting. I wasn't sure where to find meaningful connections. I forgot how much time it takes to grow those bonds. I craved it, but I also didn't know how to find it.

Ellie graduated college the same year I did, and she shared with me that her friends who got apartments and nine-to-five jobs struggled with loneliness and lack of purpose, much like I had. Meanwhile, she moved to a new city and lived in an intentional community through a volunteer program. Her job was lined up for her, she didn't have bills yet, her loans were deferred, and she had assigned, like-minded housemates. In this intentional community, no one was ever alone. They ate dinner together four nights a week. Every Monday they had a house meeting followed by a check-in when everyone took turns talking about how they were doing personally, professionally, and spiritually. They went on retreats together and did service projects once a month. These things were all required because it takes that kind of intentionality to build real community. In our busy, individualized society, when those elements aren't required, it's easy to skip them.

I wasn't required to take a turn sharing how I was doing personally, professionally, and spiritually with my roommates and co-workers, so I didn't. There were no retreats or service projects through my employer, and I didn't try to start any myself. As a strong introvert, it was too easy to just go to work, go home, and keep to myself. It felt too hard to do anything else. I was afraid of putting myself out there— who knew what might happen?

Ellie and her housemates didn't choose each other (and she said they didn't always like each other, either) but during that year, they learned to respect and love each other. She said their community felt countercultural, and it was. Creating community is hard work. It's also a little scary because it requires vulnerability. It requires a willingness to let yourself be known.

The vulnerability thing is so hard. It's so annoying. And it works. So often I pride myself on being the type of person who never needs to borrow a cup of sugar from a neighbor. You know, competent, independent, put together. Not needy. Yet there is strength in weakness. I know this. Ellie knows this. You probably know this. We get it, but we don't like it. Pain and brokenness are more than needing a cup of sugar, yet the posturing is the same. There is much to be

gained by shedding the tough person complex, remembering we don't have to do it all on our own, claiming dependence, showing weakness, leaning on community, asking for
help, allowing ourselves to be authentic and vulnerable.

> ### OTHER VOICES
>
> Lindsey has spent her adult life living in communities
> all over the US and Central America. Roles on the path
> include a residential ashram in the mountains of Colorado,
> a biodynamic farmer in Wisconsin, and a housemom for
> developmentally disabled adults. Each community contin-
> ues to inform her day-to-day life.

A week after Ellie's second child was born, he landed in
the Pediatric Intensive Care Unit, intubated for three weeks
with a nasty virus in his lungs. Her toddler was not allowed
on the floor. She said that she and her spouse took turns
switching between the hospital and home every 24 hours,
like ships passing in the night. Sleep deprived and scared,
they felt utterly vulnerable. Their community, near and far,
came out of the woodwork to hold them up. She said they
swooped in and did all the right things without being asked.
To every generous offer, they were too tired to say anything
but a grateful, "Yes, thank you." Community members
prayed, sent food, sent money, showed up unannounced,

shoveled the driveway, grocery shopped, babysat, and donated to organizations that kept kids alive. Ellie told me it was humbling and incredible. She leaned on the love of her community in her vulnerability and found sustenance. It was love in action.

About a week into the hospital stay, Ellie said that she hit a wall. Her baby had a feeding tube, so she was pumping every two hours while healing from a cesarean section. The PICU felt isolating and sterile. She wanted to hold her baby, and her supply of snacks was running low. At that point, she said a nurse walked in and told her she had a package waiting for her at the front desk. It was a basket of fruit from her intentional community friends, some of whom she had not seen in a decade. She wept. She wept because she no longer felt alone, because fruit was exactly what she wanted to eat, because they reminded her that she did not have to get through this in isolation. Her community kept her strong and fed. Years prior she dedicated a year of her life to building an intentional community with a group of strangers. The vulnerability they all brought to the shared space continued to bring life to her for years to come.

The United States is a place where the fear of scarcity and the pursuit of happiness is alive and well. Scarcity can look like not having enough money to live our preferred lifestyle, living with a low self-worth, looking to external circumstances to keep us happy, or feeling like our relationships are inadequate. It's hard to interact with others and foster a sense of community when scarcity is providing our base.

Meanwhile, our pursuit of happiness is often a solo endeavor. Happiness is presented as a choice and an inside job. If you just work harder you will make it, and then you will be happy. If we believe happiness must come from within, we turn inward, maybe reading self-help books or going to yoga to find happiness, forgetting to also turn outward to find the healing ability of community. We were made to exist in community, to come to each other's aid, solicited or not. To see past the fear of not having enough for ourselves to give a little bit to someone else. To find happiness within but also to allow other people to provide some of the foundation. We are social creatures who need community to thrive. In fact, happiness research tells us that our happiness and well-being is closely linked to the strength of our relationships to friends, family, and neighbors.

One midsummer day when my daughter was four months old, a woman pulled into our driveway and introduced herself to my husband. Aisha and her family had just moved to the area. They chatted for a few minutes, and she said she looked forward to seeing us around. A few weeks later, I packed up some veggies and walked the half mile down our shared dusty road to say hello. A man opened the door, covered in sawdust, and accepted the gift. Aisha's spouse and his father were busy gutting the house. No one else was home. That was the last we saw of them for months.

I assumed it was another failed attempt to make new adult friends. Yet early the next spring, Aisha knocked on my door.

"The house is habitable now, would you like to come over?" I brought my 15-month-old along and she played alongside Aisha's two daughters on the floor while we wrapped our hands around cups of Somali chai. I learned of her struggles with raising two young kids on top of being in graduate school, how much she wanted to have a thriving garden, and how challenging it has been to figure out how to build community in America. Growing up on another continent followed by time in a refugee camp and then several years in Europe, she knew what it was like to live in close community, where one's survival depends on one's neighbors. Despite our obvious differences, we were able to share in a way that kept me going over for tea. We didn't always laugh a lot. Some of our conversations were down-right depressing as we discussed the state of the world. But that summer we planted potatoes at my house and weeded asparagus at hers. We shared challenges and offered and accepted aid.

When my family traveled to the upper peninsula of Michigan for a vacation one year, I asked Aisha to look after the cats—giving them fresh water and food every few days. Three days into our time away, I got a text from Aisha just checking in. "Cats are fine—pouring rain here so hope you're having good weather!" We were having a good time. It was beautifully sunny. However, the fact that it was pouring rain at home was cause for concern. Our basement was prone to flooding. It's not a big deal when we are home to run the manual pump to keep it dry. But we weren't home. I started to worry about coming home to a soiled and moldy basement. It felt like an imposition to ask someone to go over and pump it out. After an hour of anxiety, I broke down and asked for help.

Aisha went over as soon as she could and manned the pump herself. The water had already started to creep into the living space, so her spouse came over, too, armed with his shop vac. What could have been a huge, expensive disaster ended in an act of kindness from a neighbor. When we pulled up to our house at the end of the week, Aisha showed up about a half hour later with a homegrown roast chicken, potatoes, and two side dishes just out of the oven. She wanted to make sure we had something decent to eat after all day in the car and a week away.

When we allow ourselves to be vulnerable and ask for help, there is always a risk. But embracing vulnerability allows us to be part of the give and take that defines being in community with the world. We call each other, heed each other, and want to know each other. That's the only way community can be born.

Knowing and being known by our neighbors is a mini revolutionary act of love. We can declare sacred ground on a chunk of land around us and commit to making sure folks who live in that shared space have what they need. Because we can create and foster community online, sometimes we get lazy about the work it requires to build community with those with whom we share physical space. There is a paradox of choice, and we forget to meet our neighbors, the people who actually live right next door. We can get groceries delivered and move business transactions onto our screens. We can cultivate relationships with folks who look and think exactly like we do in our virtual communities. We can walk into an attached garage, drive across town to work and back again without ever coming into contact with our neighbors. It's easier that way. It's faster and more predictable. It requires less vulnerability.

## OTHER VOICES

For their tenth wedding anniversary, Megan and Adam rented a room in a restaurant and treated about twenty friends to a splendid meal. After dinner, Adam toasted to their relationship and Megan toasted to the folks gathered, their found family. Each person had played a significant role in their lives, and they wanted to celebrate their couplehood and the village that feeds their love.

In a society that is structured toward isolation, we can choose to get a little vulnerable and do the work of building community for our own good. This life is not for the weary, and when the going gets tough, it takes a village. We shouldn't have to go to war to have a sense of cooperation, close quarters, and common good. We can have all of that right here. Because society nurtures individuality over vulnerability and thus isolation over community, we must engage in this subversive and life-giving work of building community. We can walk next door and risk knowing and becoming known.

## ❧ THE TINY THING ❧
### An invitation to vulnerability

Our fundamental desire as human beings is to be close to others, and our society does not allow for that.[2]
—SHARON ABRAMOWITZ

Introduce yourself to a neighbor, whom you don't yet know. Walk over to the house two doors down. When a neighbor is in the yard weeding, offer to help. Head over to the house around the corner, where the new people moved in. In order to have strong communities, we need to feel supported and needed—like we belong.

---

2. Quoted by Sebastian Junger, *Vanity Fair,* "The Bonds of Battle" (June 2015).

We need to be able to ask for help and give help when we can. It helps to have a general idea of who actually lives on our block.

Knocking on the neighbor's door is a tiny, scary act. It's not easy to put ourselves out there. But there's always a chance that the person you introduce yourself to was just waiting for you to do so. Introduce yourself to people. Make the first move. Be vulnerable and see what it brings into your community.

## Body Practice

If you are able, sit on your heels and lean forward over your thighs to place your forehead on the ground. Place your arms beside your legs so your thumbs are touching your feet. Allow your body to relax and feel your shoulder blades drift open. If this is not comfortable, curl on your right side into the fetal position and relax. Feel your weight settle into the floor. Either way, notice your smallness compared to the vast universe around you. Open yourself to a sense of vulnerability. After a few full breaths, rise with an openness, where your human limitations can be freeing instead of restricting.

## In Reflection

* How does your community feel to you right now?
* If you needed a cup of sugar, would you walk over to someone's house and ask to borrow one? Why or why not?
* What's it like to put yourself out there and ask for help? Give it?
* How are you vulnerable?
* How can you benefit from being fully invested in your immediate community?
* How can the world benefit from you being fully invested in your immediate community?
* What would change if you felt like you belonged? If you didn't?
* What is another tiny thing that could work to cultivate community in your life?

# Afterword

Happiness is not a matter of intensity but of balance, order, rhythm and harmony.[1]

—THOMAS MERTON

## Ellie

While we were putting the finishing touches on this manuscript, I was also working with a woman named Tina. Tina is a gifted bodyworker who focuses on Structural Integration through deep fascia tissue massage. The method is called Rolfing, named after Ida Rolf, the biochemist who created the technique. I saw Tina the Rolfer once a month for ten months. Each session, I felt like she was peeling

---

1. Thomas Merton, *No Man Is an Island* (Ireland: Harcourt, Brace, 2002).

away one more layer of built up gunk and inviting my inner light to shine through. She studied my body alignment and talked to me about my life while engaging in deep fascia tissue massage. Seeking out her healing was part of my quest to get in touch with and hopefully fall in love with my post-birthing body. The practice far exceeded my expectations, unlocking my entire being.

During one of my sessions, Tina was massaging my feet. They were cold, tight, and curled in on themselves. We explored where this tightness might come from. Nursing my second child was more of a struggle than my first. During feedings, I clenched my feet, expressing stress through grabbing the carpet with my toes while trying to keep my upper body still.

Tina said, "Rolfers believe that there are four energy points surrounding your body. One is 12–18 inches below your feet. One is 12–18 inches above your head, and the others are 12–18 inches to the right and left of your navel," she said. "You are a very grounded person. That groundedness is explored through your feet. We tend to work from our strengths, yet we also must find balance. Try thinking about all four points of energy. Honor your groundedness, but also acknowledge what is calling to you above your head."

I laughed aloud. I was finishing a book about nurturing my roots. I experienced having small babies as an extreme grounding, planting my life and work firmly at home. It was so fitting that at that moment, after focusing on grounding and rooting for so long, Tina reminded me to look up.

To nurture our roots, there is no one right answer. There is no destination and no arrival. There is no single direction to move, and imperfect practice is the way forward. This book is not the answer, it is a gentle reminder to tap into your roots and remember to look up, existing in the glorious tension of an ever-unfolding life.

Heidi and I placed the learning and community chapters last for that very reason. We both find a great deal of meaning in deepening our roots, but we never want to grow complacent even in that good work. There is always a new balance to be struck, tension to live in, energy calling to us from above as we delve deeper. And we don't do it alone. We need deep roots to weather the storms of life, and we also need to lift our gaze regularly to marvel at how our resilient branches can bend in the wind. There is new learning to be done, a new edge to explore, a new direction to turn. The work is not just for us, but for the wholeness of our communities. Nature thrives with diversity, in relation to the web of life, and that extends to human creatures as well. When we move beyond ourselves into our community. The journey is as complex as our beings. We hope you found a gift or two to place in your satchel for the next stretch of road.

# Acknowledgments

This project has been unfolding for a while and will continue in our lives long after today. Little things will always be big things. Intentionality will always be part of our path to wholeness. Several years ago, a group of lovely and wise women gathered to ask the question, "What is enough?" Suan Vaughn-Fier, Emily McKinley, Kris Woll, Claire De Berg, Kate Percuoco, Michelle Johnson, Erin Benson, and Mary Beth Owen offered their voices to that layered, rich conversation. Thank you for laying the foundation for this book. Kris Woll in particular was a priceless thought partner as *Enough* became *12 Tiny Things*. We are grateful.

We started the 12 Tiny Things group on Facebook and watched, amazed, as it took root, grew, and is now thriving. The community grounds us, inspires us, holds us accountable, and is the living, breathing, three-dimensional heartbeat and soul of this book. To our 12 Tiny Things family, you support us in surprising and incredible ways and make the detailed slogfest of publishing a book oh so worth it. We are better together. Thank you to all the folks who took time to share their stories in these pages and with the online community group. If these chapters have vibrancy it is because of the texture your particular and intentional lives add. Thank you for being such generous thought partners and for letting us see tiny things in action.

Birthing a book takes hope and hard work, artistry and attention to detail, inspiration and willpower. It is no small feat and no one does it alone. We have the very best team and feel so lucky to work with our agent, Dawn Frederick, our editor, Lisa Kloskin, and our Broadleaf Books family including Rachel Reyes, Mallory Hayes, and Emily Benz. Whitney Stofflet and Kristie Nelson-Neuhaus, your talent, creativity, and support elevated the project and made it sing. Your friendship made creation way more fun. We were repeatedly struck by our luck to have all these incredibly competent, invested, and kind women at the table.

I, Ellie, would like to thank my mother, Margie, and mother-in-law, Janet. It is such a joy and privilege to drop my boys off with you so they can laugh and play and learn from you while I write. You love them so well and make me brave enough to keep creating while parenting. Simon and Miles, your creativity and imagination, your love of stories, and your pure presence invite me to live in the essence of wonder and delight. You remind me daily to joyfully embrace each tiny, fleeting moment. Dan, you continue to be the living definition and embodiment of the word *partner*. I can write and live out my value of tiny things because of your engagement in our family and the love, stability, and presence you offer daily. I love the life we are building. Your shoulder remains my favorite place to find rest. Bethlehem Lutheran Church Twin Cities and Louisville Institute—thank you for believing in me and this project and backing that up with the gift of time and funds. I am deeply grateful for the lively and loving communities that sustain me, inspire me, and offer me grace: Up Yoga, The Loft, The Global Immersion Project, The Collegeville Institute, and Riverside Innovation Hub.

Thank you to my brilliant, generous and utterly lovely writing mentors Jo Ann Beard and Verlyn Klinkenborg. Thank you to Mary Hess for believing in my potential when my work was shaky. Juliet, thank you for your friendship and photos. Catherine Hull, thank you for your steadfast love and commitment to feeding me art like bread. Thank you to my friends and fellow writers Sally Franson, Caren Stelson, Stina Kielsmeier-Cook, Laura Kelly Fanucci, Meta Herrick Carlson, and Emmy Kegler for being true to your craft and supporting me in mine. Ellen Weber, Emma Almeroth, Juliet Farmer, and Matthew Ian Fleming—collaborating with you makes my heart sing.

And Heidi Barr, thank you. You are a dream-come-true creative partner. Your intelligence matches your goodness. Your work ethic matches your expertise. Writing a book is hard. Co-writing a book with a friend could have been a complete and utter disaster. Instead, because of you, it continues to be a life-giving project I deeply believe in.

―――――――

I, Heidi, would like to thank my health coaching colleagues Holly Walsh and Julie Wild for your constant fellowship, through all sorts of ups and downs, during the last decade. Our conversations over the years have helped shape my coaching practice, my personal life, and how I write about all of it. Thank you to the fine folks at Noom for your continual and enthusiastic support of my writing life, especially Andreas Michaelides, Maryn Fulton, Carrie Berry, Rachel McGinnis, and the rest of the coaching team—it's good to be a part of the Noomily. I appreciate your passion and commitment to equipping people with the tools and support they need to thrive. Thank you to Leslie Browning and the Homebound Publications circle of authors for being an essential part of my life as a writer. Thank you to Rebecca Long, Catherine Birkelo, and Kifah Abdi for your friendship and support with whatever I'm working on or through.

Ellie Roscher, thank you for being the absolute best person on the planet with whom to co-write a book—I am so grateful for your partnership with this project. It's what it is because of how committed you are to the things that matter to you and the way you show up in the world grounded, with love for life as a guiding force.

To my parents, siblings, and extended family: thank you for all the ways, from huge to tiny, that you offer support, guidance, and love. Eva, thank you for the lessons you continue to teach me by being a curious learner and approaching each day with an open heart and mind. And Nick, thank you for being an integral part of my root system and for always reminding me to go outside and look up. I'm so grateful to experience this life alongside you.

———

Finally, to you, our readers, thank you for being our co-travelers on the journey. May your roots be nourished so that you can rise.

# Appendix

## Additional Ideas for Tiny Things

### Space / Enough

Try a Nothing Day: stay home and offline, letting the day of relaxation unfold.

Start a wellness calendar to prioritize things that bring you life.

When you feel yourself slipping into an old, cluttered mental commentary, ask yourself if the story you are telling yourself is true. Hit pause and create space for a true story.

Donate ten things that don't bring you joy.

Block space on your calendar once a week just for you.

Show up to things early on purpose with no agenda and see what happens.

Pick one daily activity, like putting lotion on your hands or walking a certain staircase, and do it very slowly. Don't rush. Take up space.

## Work / Presence

Shut down your work computer at the end of the day. When you return to the screen, take a few deep breaths as your computer is starting back up.

A few times during your workday, do a tiny body practice. Take note of your posture. Roll your shoulders back and reach the crown of your head up. Feel the chair against your back or your feet on the floor.

Put something in your workspace that reminds you of what you value most in life.

Charge your phone at night away from your bedroom.

Make a list of the things you would do if you didn't need money. Make sure to incorporate some of these things into your life.

Put on a CD or record and really pay attention to every step of getting the music to play. Then listen to at least one song beginning to end.

Before using a machine like your computer, car, or coffee maker, give it a nod of gratitude in recognition of how it brings ease to your life.

Identify three things you enjoy about your work, paid or not.

## Spirituality / Attention

Light a candle every day at the same time.

Set an alarm on your phone or calendar to alert you twice a day. When it does, pause and direct your attention to something that makes you feel alive. Focus on it for ten seconds, give it thanks, and then move on.

Next time you wash the dishes, do it by hand, and wash the dishes as though it were a sacred act.

Create a new ritual for yourself or your family.

Watch the sun rise or set once a week.

Set an intention for your day. Maybe it's one word, the name of a person, or an issue. When you become conscious of your breath, return to your intention to get centered.

## Food / Alchemy

Once a week, set aside enough time to mindfully prepare a meal. Hold the food. Smell the meal at each stage. Taste often. Play music or pour a glass of wine.

Prepare a meal with only one food like rice, potatoes, or bread. Allow the lack of variety to raise your attention around food disparity. Consider donating the money saved.

Pick one food to source locally.

Sit down when you eat.

Start a food swap. Gather up a few neighbors and agree to meet once every couple months to trade whatever bounty you've got—from veggies to cookies to soup.

As you cook, really notice how ingredients come together to transform into something else.

Eat your snack with your eyes closed.

Let your favorite treat dissolve in your mouth and really savor it.

Make your full plate a work of art—a gorgeous arrangement of tasty food.

## Style / Alignment

Pick one object and build around that. Pick a pair of shoes you love and build an outfit. Pick a rug and build a room. Pick a T-shirt or an album cover and use just those colors and feelings as a filter.

Write down five to seven words that you want your room/wardrobe/etc. to embody.

Ensure you feel alignment with what you are wearing. Put clothes that don't make your heart sing aside. Ask your friends to swap clothes. Donate what doesn't get swapped.

Wear something that truly feels like "me."

Wear something that feels out of character—notice how it feels.

Pick an accessory like a bracelet or certain pair of socks that you choose to infuse with gratitude. On days when you need it, wear gratitude.

## Nature / Wildness

Pick up a piece of nature—a fallen branch, a colorful leaf or plush flower—and bring it inside.

Lie on the grass and watch the clouds go by.

Walk barefoot to get the mail from the mailbox.

Find an outside spot where you can sit or meander around, undisturbed. Get to know it in all seasons.

Get to know a tree. Put your hands on its bark, smell it, notice its rootedness.

Wander in a park.

Observe birds or squirrels for ten minutes.

## Communication / See

Pick a room in your house to place your phone and keep it there.

Pick someone in your family. Take two to three minutes and imagine their day from hour to hour. Imagine what life might be like for someone else, and let that vision inform how you interact. Repeat regularly.

Pick one day a month to keep your phone off all day.

Try replacing your "I'm sorry," with "Thank you." So, instead of, "I'm sorry I'm late," try "Thank you for your patience."

Do a social media detox. Let people know you won't be checking online for any stretch of time you choose.

Open up space for empathy by asking, "What is it like to be you?"

Notice one nonverbal/non-written way you communicate.

We get asked, "How are you?" several times a day. Choose a narrative that infuses your communication with grateful light. Repeating that story throughout your day can change your lens to one of abundance. For example, instead of, "I am really busy and stressed," try, "My life is rich and full right now," or "I'm humming at a high vibration, and it's exciting."

## Home / Gratitude

Take a month and try a spending freeze, buying nothing new outside of necessities. Think critically about what you need and how you value money and things.

Nurture a houseplant.

Rearrange the furniture in one of your rooms. Notice what happens when you have a fresh look and perspective.

Write down the things you like about your living space.

Put a journal on your nightstand. Either first thing in the morning or last thing at night (or both!) take a few moments to write down the good stuff.

Change the pictures in your frames. A new picture will catch your eye. Choose photos of people, places, and moments that you are grateful for.

Use bright Post-it notes to write down some people and things for which you are thankful. Post them in places that you will see during the day like your bathroom mirror, refrigerator, rearview mirror, and computer screen.

Choose a candle that will represent your gratitude. Light it during a meal or while you are working. Intentionally reflect.

Go to a place in your neighborhood you've never been to before. A different place every day. Start seeing the familiar with new eyes.

Choose a vase and put paper and a pen by it. Whenever a moment happens that brings gratitude, write it down and put it in the vase. Then choose a time once a week or on Thanksgiving or New Year's to read them aloud.

## Sensuality / Desire

Try Brené Brown's idea of writing permission slips for yourself. "I grant you permission to have fun today." Write it on a Post-it note and carry it with you.

Buy a perfume or aromatherapy scent. Once a day, put a drop behind both ears, close your eyes, and take a deep breath in. Notice what happens to your thoughts and body.

Once a week, carve out a time to prioritize your body. Pamper your own body. Take a warm bath. Try a face mask. Curl up under a blanket in a ball and cry. Stretch. Be tender with your body, address it like a long-lost friend.

Take a moment to listen to your voice. Make lots of different and weird sounds with your voice. Find space and expansion within the sounds your voice can make. How does your voice take up space in the world?

Physically experiment with being small and then large. Make yourself into a ball. Spread your arms and legs wide. Notice how it feels.

Wear black or gray one day and a loud pattern the next. Speak quietly one day and laugh loudly the next. Reflect on how these changes make you feel.

Give up something you love (like honey in coffee) for a week to experience it anew when it returns.

Pay attention to the times you feel most stressed and simply notice what they are.

Pay attention to your posture/body space in various situations.

Set an alarm to remind yourself to pay attention to how your body is feeling at a given moment.

Really listen to what your body wants to do and go do it.

## Creativity / Start

Set aside time once a month to be creative with other people. Gather a group of friends with the intention of being creative together.

Create a "room of your own" in your home. Whether it's a corner or a full room, make it your special spot to unleash your creativity.

Finger paint. Color. Stack some blocks. Get back to the basics of what you enjoyed creating as a small child. See what it feels like to revisit this as an adult.

Cooking dinner? Artfully arrange the finished product on serving platters.

Mowing the lawn? Make patterns with the mower.

Picking up the kids from school? Play your favorite music and sing along on the drive.

## Learning / Curiosity

If your day typically ends with television, try listening to an audiobook to break the muscle memory of picking up the remote.

Sign up for a community education class.

Go to an author talk, poetry reading, or presentation at your local bookshop or library.

Make a list of the books you want to read. Request one at the library.

Get a stack of back issue *National Geographic*. Flip through and learn something new!

Each morning commit to being open to surprise. Each evening, reflect on what surprised you that day.

## Community / Vulnerability

Notice one thing you need and ask someone for help.

Volunteer at a community meal or help out at the food shelf.

Attend your local street dance, block night out, or festival.

Next time you have a few days off, take a "staycation" and explore your immediate neighborhood on foot or on a bike.

Go for a walk around your neighborhood and make a point to say hello to at least three people.

Sit on your front porch or in your front yard. Say hello to a passerby.

Attend a local town hall meeting.